Safe From the Storm

Healing the Wounds from Your Loved
One's Addiction

Jenny Kennedy

Kennedy Literary Agency

Special Thanks to:

IBrandlt Digital – Lu Anderson

Raven Mad Productions – Cassandra Hinnegan

Cover Photo by: Colin Lloyd

Contents

Dedication

This book is dedicated to my loved ones.
May addiction never find its grip again,
and may deep healing bring you to great happiness.
This book is also dedicated to the woman who loved so
bravely and finally found just as much love for herself,
as she did her loved ones.

Introduction

Welcome friends. I am grateful you are here and very sorry that life has been hard for you and your loved one. Safe from the Storm is written for you and your healing while respecting your loved one's situation.

This book landed in your hands for a reason. Whether you bought it or got it as a gift, the Universe has found a way to deliver some messages to you. Perhaps you have been ignoring them, or maybe you were praying for some help. Either way, you needed something to change.

Because let's face it, addiction is so painful! We don't know how to stop it. Addiction robs us of our mothers, fathers, sons, daughters, sisters, brothers, aunts, uncles, grandparents, and friends. The fallout is severe. Our loved ones go to unbelievable lengths to maintain their addiction until they are ready to enter recovery. It twists them into unrecognizable imitations of the people we knew and loved.

And guess who follows suit? Us.

Addiction is an ugly cycle with many layers to it— like a jawbreaker. Only it is a family breaker. Until someone cuts the restraints of their habits to face the underlying pain, addiction wins. As family and friends, we think that the only way this craziness will stop is for The Addicted to get sober. We don't believe that we have issues and unhealthy habits ourselves as a by-product. That's right. You can break the cycle of addiction by changing how you participate in it.

You may be in a state of sheer panic and terror. But, on the other hand, you may be resigned to living with the addiction going on in your loved one's life. Maybe your loved one is very sick. Maybe they are in treatment or newly sober. Maybe they have passed away, or you have just realized they have a problem. Maybe you are in denial or keenly aware of what is going on. Maybe you are a child of addiction who is struggling to break coping behavior. Perhaps you are at the end of your rope. Whatever stage you are at right now, I want you to know that I have been there too. And because there are so many others like us, you should know you are not alone.

Addiction is so very isolating for The Addicted and The Affected. Society is slow to come around to a compassionate approach to addiction, and there is a multitude of shaming and judgment preventing people from getting the proper help they need.

It's entirely understandable to be feeling everything you are experiencing right now. It's okay to feel conflicted and confused. It's okay to be furious. It's okay to think (insert addiction of choice) is an absolute bullshit excuse to use as an escape from life's problems. However, wherever you are right now, you will move forward using this book, one step at a time.

You are safe here. You are safe to reflect. You are safe to feel. You are safe to move away from shame and guilt. You can allow forgiveness for yourself because you did the best you could and trust that there is a way out. Allow yourself the space to be in the moment with me as you read through each chapter. Give the practices your attention and complete them as an act of self-love. When it gets scary or overwhelming, allow yourself to feel into the moment instead of stuffing it down. And when you need a break— pause for some peace and your trusted healthy self-care practice.

It's time to let go of everything you held on to so tightly and let it flow out of you.

When you have a loved one in addiction, you learn coping mechanisms to regulate your life around it. Regardless of loved ones being fully immersed, recently recovered, or in sobriety, you learned ways to ease the pain and keep some form of sanity to prevent imploding yourself.

So first, I will point out that there is no fault or shame in how you've coped with your loved one's addiction in the past. It is heart-wrenchingly painful to witness addiction rob someone you love of their health, relationships, employment, and mental wellbeing. It's a loss like no other. You feel helpless, and you likely tried everything in your power to turn the ship around before it hit the rocks. You've done your best, and that was all you could do.

Now it's time to do something different— better. Looking after yourself now releases the pressure of caretaking and shows your loved one the example of a healthy life. It improves your relationships, too.

Second, you couldn't know the right thing to do while you were in the cycle of addiction. The eye of the storm is a terrifying place. Not until you learn to step outside of it, that is. Once you determine your boundaries and your own needs, you can decide what tips to use and which to discard. If it works for you, keep doing it. There is no judgment or shame here. You can act in your best interests without feeling guilty or abandoning your own needs.

I know first-hand what addiction does to loved ones and their families. Unfortunately, addiction doesn't just rob our loved ones of precious time; it robs us too. We can become just as obsessed as they are as it takes over our lives until we also experience poor health, problems at work, broken relationships, and financial struggles.

It can be an ugly process to heal and live our lives despite what our loved ones are going through. Yet, once you find your stride, I assure you that it is possible to find happiness regardless of their situation. I'm not saying you won't hurt or struggle, but you will move back into balance when difficult problems occur with some practice. The more proficient you are, the sooner you release the grip of caretaking, appeasing, and attempting to control the outcome.

The only control we have is reacting to the circumstances life throws at us and forming an action plan. The stronger your self-care practice and the more you use the tools in your toolbox, the more manageable the challenges. It may not be perfect. It can still be a little messy at times, but with the skills and exercises in this book, you will have a new mindset to turn to time and again.

Why I Wrote This Book

Have you noticed that addiction gets an awful lot of attention? Our loved one is constantly in some kind of crisis, and we have spent a great deal of time doing damage control. I sure did. For over fifteen years, addiction spiraled through my relationships, upending my goals and clouding my judgment.

Addiction doesn't leave a lot of room for families, friends, and spouses. We lose focus on our purpose in life, our dreams and goals slowly disappearing while trying to save someone from their damaging behaviors.

I wrote this book to help people bring their attention to where it belongs— with you.

The journey through self-awareness and nourishing self-care practices got me through the most challenging years of my life. If I hadn't refocused my attention on myself, the cycle would have continued until I got very sick, and I was already too close to that fire to carry on the same way. Something had to change within, and the person I needed to save was me.

By sharing my story and the steps I took to get healthy again, I hope to help others find the way out of their role in addiction and back into fully living their lives.

Thank you for investing your time and money in your healing journey. Thank you for hearing my story and holding space for me. Thank you for allowing me to hold space for you.

I now set the intention of this book to bring
understanding, a lightening of the load, a place
of sharing, awareness, love, and healing

for ourselves so that our loved ones in
addiction can see the value in doing the same
for themselves.

Preface

How to Use the Book

This book is a judgment-free zone. You won't find finger-pointing or shaming on these pages. Too much of that has become the norm around addiction and causes more damage than good. You also won't find a bunch of psychology jargon. My intention is to be less formal and more personal.

In the spirit of creating a healing space, I have refused to use labels like addict, codependent, alcoholic, enabler, or any other terms used to define people. They are behaviors, not who we are. We are all people— human. Consequently, I believe these terms remove humanity from the topic of addiction, and these classifications limit a person's ability to heal. Unfortunately, I think society finds these labels acceptable, and we don't realize their impact.

Instead, to borrow from Dr. Gabor Mate, I will use The Addicted for our loved ones and The Affected for us. These terms accurately describe the relative situation. We must create a gentle space to process our feelings, lessen the sharp edges, and the cutting words to heal. Sure, we used various tactics and behaviors to manage an impossible situation, and those actions would be termed codependent— and it is a real thing, don't get me wrong.

First, I intend to point you in the right direction. Then, once you have momentum, you can further your healing journey with professionals specializing in codependent behaviors and boundary setting. This book is your guide to a self-empowered healing experience on your terms.

I will include a list of other experts, counselors, therapists, coaches, and healers at the end of this book. If you are interested in purchasing their books, I have a link to my reading list on my author's website, www.jennykennedy.ca.

This book breaks old thought patterns and behaviors with provoking information, writing exercises, and affirmations. Each chapter moves you through another step until, finally, you focus more on what makes you happy and less on your loved one's condition.

Here is what you will need:

-Make sure you have one or two beautiful spiral-bound journals and a favorite pen. Get ones that feel heavenly to use.

-Meditation pillow or cushion, one that allows you to be comfortable when you are sitting on the floor.

-Thick yoga mat. It is for under your meditation cushion so that your legs, ankles, and feet are comfortable but also so that you can lay down if you have trouble sitting up at first.

-A cozy throw blanket that you save just for meditation or self-care time. Sometimes you can get cold while meditating. Set the intention that you are receiving a loving hug every time you use it.

Please Note:

I am writing from my perception and don't speak for my family or loved ones. Specific details have been omitted to maintain their privacy. The reality is while I may find it therapeutic and helpful to share my story, my loved ones would likely suffer the opposite, and I don't want to be responsible for mental anguish or, worse, trigger a setback.

I don't pretend to be a counselor, therapist, or represent medical advice. Instead, I am sharing my thoughts and experience with addiction and practices that worked for my healing. If you become overwhelmed, unable to cope, or need additional support at any point, I urge you to reach out for professional help. It is the most powerful form of self-care there is, and you deserve just as much attention as your loved one does.

While you are reading, keep in mind that we all have different terms for God. I use Universe. So please insert what resonates with you, whether it is God, Higher Power, Inner Being, Source, or Soul. All are welcome. No one is telling you what to believe. The idea is to start thinking and expanding on what is your own belief, so don't allow any single person's language, belief system, or religion to cause any pause.

You will also find 'Jenny Truths' throughout the book. These are moments where I discovered something monumental for myself. These are not affirmations, though you will find those too. Instead, Jenny Truths are realizations, moments of clarity, honest assessments, and awareness that allow fresh perspective where I was stuck before.

When it is time to do the writing exercises, you will find the instructions and questions featured, so they are easy to find.

Relax as much as possible while you read. It is your time. Find a comfy spot and wrap yourself in your cozy blanket.

I am so glad you are here! Let's get started.

Chapter One

My Story

Addiction is a wild tornado. It spins out of control, flinging debris large and small with the power to take out homes, businesses, families, and friends. Instead of getting out of its path, we jumped into the eye of the storm with The Addicted doing everything possible to get them to stop. We became just as trapped as they are without a way back out.

It is no secret that substance abuse is a rampant problem in the world today. But, of course, there are many forms of addiction, and people often suffer from more than one at the same time. Every addiction ruins relationships, health, careers, and finances.

It isn't a stretch that with millions of people suffering from addiction, that number multiplies significantly because of the friends and family who suffer with them. Without self-awareness, healing, and support, the cycle of addiction will continue to tear apart our lives.

In truth, the real problem is unresolved trauma. Of course, it's different for everyone; however, using substances or other means are all designed to feel ANYTHING BUT the repressed pain. If you haven't discovered Gabor Mate and his teachings, I highly encourage you to do so. See the back of this book. It resonated so strongly with what I experienced and my outlook on life. His teachings also gave me peace that my perspective on addiction wasn't naive or silly. Unfortunately, I didn't discover his work until years later.

My Story

My journey with my loved ones' addiction includes four people in my life. I was extremely close to three of them, while the fourth was indirect but catastrophic. One died. Two are in sobriety, and one continues to struggle. One was on death's door more than once, but I convinced them to get help before it was too late. One, I had to exercise every boundary in my arsenal to function. With three, I had to put the wellbeing of children first, despite how much it broke my heart to do it. And, I've had to remove a child and get legal custody to protect them from neglect and abandonment. Alcohol, marijuana, and prescription drugs fueled their addictions, but gambling and porn addictions were also present.

Viewing a loved one's addiction from the front row has a different perspective than the nose bleed section. Up close, you are privy to the minute details, but you can't see the entire scene so well. Farther back, you see the bigger picture, but you don't always understand the intimate details, and your imagination is left to fill in the blanks.

I've been in both the front row and the gallery. It's like an aquarium whale show where the orcas purposely splash the audience. It didn't matter where I was sitting. I got soaking wet and couldn't escape the tidal wave coming my way. But, of course, up close was way worse.

I struggled in a sea of work, family responsibilities, several life-threatening situations, and mental health diagnoses. Looking back, I have no idea how I didn't have a mental breakdown sooner. But, unfortunately, I broke down after everyone else was safe, my relationship ended, and I had more than enough time to feel the full-force impact finally.

I feel like I have lived multiple lifetimes already. Each had hope, laughter, fun, blessings, and tremendous love. But, there was also loss, death, chaos, hardship, and indescribable pain... all because of my loved ones' addictions.

Substance abuse is a matter of life and death, sometimes stretched over years and other times stopped short by an overdose. While I know many people who lost their children to overdoses, my loved ones' addictions were years in the making. Unfortunately, it leaves a lot of room for doubt, second-guessing, and denial because there is still hope if they aren't dead. That fear is a powerful motivator, but fear feeds on itself and pulls you to the very depths until you can't hold your breath any longer.

That's a lot of metaphors, but I think you get the drift. Here is one more. Substance abuse is the poor attempt at a life raft when a person is drowning in pain. Take the life raft away, and they panic, lashing out in a desperate attempt to survive at all cost. If you get in the water with them, you run the risk of being pulled under too. Ah, but if they learn to swim, they rebuild their strength and stop relying on substances. I knew this. I knew it so well that I spent years treading water beside them, showing them the strokes and how to kick, but I almost drowned after exhaustion set in. But any sign I broke through enticed me to keep going.

The idea of saving people is a noble one. Hope can be addicting. I got hooked on relief when it seemed my loved one finally heard me. Hope kept me in the cycle of addiction with them and ultimately left me utterly devastated. I was physically and emotionally worn out, and my health was on the line.

The Roots Run Deep

Every person on this planet learns a unique cocktail of problem-solving, coping, human connections, tastes, mannerisms, and survival skills from early childhood. Parents, siblings, relatives, friends, teachers, coaches, and lovers play a part throughout our lives, but certain things originate from birth. Personality types differ, even amongst siblings, as do attachment styles, making our decision-making, conflict management, and relationship-building skills distinctive to each person.

As children, we learn how to navigate the world from our parents and caretakers, and we continue to glean strategies as we carry on in life. Our childhoods could be filled with beautiful memories or tarnished with disfunction. Either way, we grow up with tools in our toolbox— whether they help or hinder us.

Some people don't have great childhoods or role models, so they do their best to fill in the blanks without healthy fundamental skills to maneuver in life. And others have never experienced any hardship to navigate difficulties. Or something in between the two. Either way, we are all learning and finding ways to evolve through life's challenges.

Children who grew up with one or both parents in addiction learn a unique set of survival skills. So do abused children, whether physical, mental, emotional, or sexual. They may not know life any other way and believe it to be normal. Still, these kids certainly learned how to avoid trouble, appease their parents by any means necessary, disappear if possible, or instigate trouble to end the tension. Those are just a few examples. But when people don't have anyone to help them, no one to connect with or hear their pain, they become deeply traumatized from their experiences.

I learned at an early age not to share my feelings, get mad or speak up for myself because if I did, there were unpleasant consequences. Eventually, I would blow up, which often meant that I was the problem instead of my feelings. So instead, I tried to do everything right, avoiding trouble to the extreme that I only felt valued when I did a good job or made someone feel good. Yet, whatever I did, it wasn't quite enough to fill the connection I was seeking. So I learned to be even better, try harder, prove myself to every person I came across. Thus, my caretaking, codependent behaviors were born.

It comes down to connection. We are humans, and connecting with other humans is how we learn and grow, to feel safe and relate to our surroundings. Without that connection, a cord breaks, and trauma is born. Disconnection causes trauma from the underlying belief that we aren't worthy of the love, affection, and attention that is in our very nature to crave. We learn how to parent from our parents or lack thereof, and unhealthy behavior passes down through generations. Until there is a break in the line of thinking, the same lessons get passed down through our children. Whether it was abusive or not, the depth of that trauma depends on the unique events each of us experiences growing up.

I was fortunate to grow up on our family farm, surrounded by great people and all sorts of animals. Taking care of each other, working hard, honesty, loyalty, and love were mottos we lived by, and my childhood was blessed. Of course, we had our fair share of difficulties. I can't say I learned how to manage conflict well, but for the most part, I'd say I was somewhat sheltered from most of life's harshness.

Naively, I assumed most people were like my family. It wasn't until my teens and early twenties that I discovered otherwise, and my 'fixing' began.

Thinking of a career in psychology, I decided to volunteer for the local sexual assault center and see if that field was a good fit. It wasn't that I didn't know about abuse or rape before that, but it takes on a whole new meaning when you are talking to an attack victim at three in the morning and organizing services for them. Unfortunately, some of the horror stories were enough to weaken the strongest resolve, leaving me too shaken to pursue psychology any further. Still, those events happened to someone else, not me, and while I used those skills in other ways, it didn't truly hit home until it involved my loved ones.

My ability to empathize with people is a gift. Deep down, my nature is to help by whatever means possible. If I weren't able to help, I would find someone or something that could.

So if I look plainly at my past, my caretaking, hardworking, loving personality went into overdrive whenever a loved one's situation appeared dire. This tendency drew me to people who needed help the most, perhaps because it made me feel good to do it. That in itself is addicting, a moral reward for seeing the bigger truth and having an answer to their problem. But, unfortunately, it also made me susceptible to being taken advantage of when people didn't do the work themselves.

Without a solid conflict navigation system, I didn't know how to say no or ask for what I needed without fear of a negative consequence or sounding critical. The harder I worked and the more solutions I provided meant I was more valuable— or so I thought. My ability to be responsible, take charge, and get things done made it very easy for people to slack off and let me handle it. Worse was being praised for my efforts because they made me feel appreciated. So I did even more, and I lost track of my own goals for the sake of being needed. I was in the codependency cycle for a long time because of my supercharged caretaking habits.

On the flip side, my loved ones had several issues that caused them pain, anxiety, mental illness, heartbreak, and control issues. It was comforting to have someone like me understand their problems, and it felt better to have someone taking care of them. In some cases, they were neglected or abused as a child, and others suffered mental conditions that made day-to-day life feel impossible without someone managing it for them. I was a comfort when they had so little.

My loved ones' actions weren't malicious or consciously manipulative. I would say all of them were in survival mode to varying degrees. But someone was treading water with them, and it felt a hell of a lot better than being alone in deep water without knowing how to swim. So how they learned to cope was second nature to them, and until someone came along to show them differently, or something drastic happened, my loved ones would continue down the same path.

And there I was—that someone. Egotistically, I thought I knew the way. It did, in fact, save my loved one's life more than once. But, whatever I thought, my heart was in the right place no matter how clumsily I pulled it off.

Witnessing Addiction

As a friend or family member watching our loved ones wither away, killing themselves on their substance of choice, it rots our guts out and makes us crazy to feel so helpless. But mainly because they seem blindly unaware (though they know very well). The Addicted raise absolute hell with anyone who tries to talk sense into them or appease us with promises that they will seek help just to get us out of their face. Other times, they weave a convincing story before stealing belongings to sell for drug money or pay off debts. So we have three options: do something to help them (which feels better for us short term), create an authentic conversation with boundaries (whether they are willing to participate or not), or walk away and leave them to figure it out on their own.

I have done all three. But, I was overactive on the 'do something' part. In some cases, I had to act for the sake of a child's safety, but in others, the lines got blurred between what was necessary and what was taking over someone else's work. Walking away was the worse feeling in the world, so it was only natural that I avoided that until I couldn't choose anything else. So, when I finally learned about healthy boundaries, it was a relief to know I was doing what was best for my loved ones and me and also very confusing. Setting boundaries and sticking to them felt selfish or mean, which led to guilt. Again, it didn't feel good, so I avoided that too. But then, when I couldn't do otherwise, I realized I was gifting myself peace and trusted that my loved one benefited from the hard lesson too.

When you love someone deeply, you feel their pain just as deeply. With substance abuse or any addiction, we think this is something they are doing to themselves. The answer? They should just stop it! And if they don't, they deserve punishment and the consequences of their actions. But if we felt the extent of the pain they were in for the same length of time, not only would we likely resort to [insert addiction here], but we would have far more empathy for them too. Instead, watching it is simply unbearable, and we use our unique coping skills to avoid it. It hurts so much!

I'm what you would call a 'doer.' I learned this from my parents. Between my loving nature, work ethic, and experience at the assault center, I felt destined to help people heal. If I could lessen their pain and make them see life from a new perspective, then not only would they get better, but I wouldn't have to worry or hurt for them anymore. The only way I would feel better was their recovery, but it gave them all the power until I finally ran out of steam.

Relief is a deep instinct, and we will always seek it out. Without awareness and the bravery to ask ourselves why we will continue to blunder in the cause and effect of addiction and codependent behaviors.

My Path Through Addiction

Sharing draws attention to harrowing memories, shining a light on things I couldn't touch for over two years. Writing about them set off triggers, bad dreams, and many tears to the point I had to stop. When I was ready to try again, I realized I poured my guts out onto hundreds of pages, but what I wrote was thrashing through unresolved trauma that needed more healing. Finally, I managed to edit myself and look at the past with more gentleness and forgiveness.

There are still moments that bring me to rage, and if I could, I would blow up what happened and rearrange the pieces in a different order. Life doesn't work that way, but I was that desperate and hurt. Yet, other moments remind me of great love and the strength I've gained through clarity.

Gabor Mate describes people as 'The Addicted' and 'The Affected.' It isn't about labels or finger-pointing but rather what we experience because of the pain behind addiction. And it resonates with me. So, to borrow Gabor's terms, I will highlight my journey without particulars on who I'm talking about or where these events happened.

The Addicted in my life suffered from various forms of abuse, sexual assault, depression, anxiety, mental disorders (diagnosed and undiagnosed), grief, neglect, abandonment, kidnapping, oppression, manipulation, thoughts of suicide, and generational issues. It led to drinking, gambling, sex/pornography, and drug addictions from significant to severe, along with multiple coping mechanisms to avoid addressing the underlying trauma and pain. Lying, stealing, manipulating, acting, saying all the right things, hiding, raging, threatening, accusing, denying... they did it all to maintain some level of their comfort zone. As a result, they lost jobs, homes, relationships, businesses, financial security, custody of children, health, and worse— their life.

Three of my loved ones were hospitalized on multiple occasions, including in psychiatric wards, for weeks and sometimes months. Two should never have walked out of the hospital again. Two needed liver transplants but wouldn't qualify due to their addictions. Three went to addiction treatment centers, with one going through detox and treatment five times. One of them included a family retreat where I learned about codependency and boundaries for the first time. Three of them lost custody or access to their children. Three experienced evictions and three became homeless.

Of the four loved ones in addiction, two have been in sobriety for over a year, one continues to struggle, and one died of alcohol-related organ failure. All of them have felt the deepest of despair, utterly alone in their pain with no foreseeable end in sight, and they did their best to survive. All refused to get help on multiple occasions, denying their problems until they hit rock bottom. They weren't as alone in their pain as they thought, though, and the people who loved them most suffered too.

The Affected were many, not just myself. We suffered anxiety, depression, neglect, denial, avoidance, dishonesty, abuse, grief, suicidal thoughts, codependency, and generational issues. There are a lot of similarities between the experiences and coping techniques of The Addicted's, making addiction a very complex issue tied together with trauma.

We also learned to deny, lie, cover up, make excuses, rant, rave, beg, ignore, appease, and problem-solve in an attempt to save both our loved ones and ourselves further pain. I did all of these things. The more normal I could make things seem, the less people bothered me or my loved one, and the more I could function. I certainly know that The Addicted did the same with their parents' addictions or abuse. The worse things got, the harder I had to work at the façade until I eventually gave out. My breakdown didn't happen when I was in the eye of the tornado; it came when the debris fell, and I stood there alone in the aftermath.

I've watched The Addicted in my life become walking skeletons still denying their drinking problem. I've planned my loved one's funeral for the sake of their children with no idea what I was doing. I've refused to allow psychiatrists to discharge my loved one and insisted on further assessments. I've argued with doctors who gave up on my loved ones. I've denied my feelings to keep the peace even when my loved one demanded all my time and attention. I've made it to the hospital just in time to witness my loved one's death. I've organized painful interventions with friends and family to convince a loved one to go to treatment. I've received phone calls from police and hospitals that my loved one was in trouble or not expected to survive. I've watched my loved one fall into addiction after surviving their parent's addiction since they were a child. I've taken custody of my loved one's child after being kidnapped and then abandoned. I've seen children neglected to the point of missing school, mental distress, massive anxiety, and physical illness. I've had items go missing and know others did too. I've stood in courtrooms, hospital rooms, psych wards, hallways, streets, and businesses while silently screaming my head off.

I learned to search the house to find an alarming amount of paraphernalia and bottles, which was always worse when I caught them in a lie. I learned to catch them in the act. I've been called names and blamed for family problems when I implemented boundaries and consequences. I've watched families not know what to do, so did nothing. I've watched families try to do something but got it wrong and caused a lot of damage. I've acted out of panic and regrettably taken it out on my kids. I've given customers shit for gossiping and poor behavior in defense of my loved one. I've quietly cleaned up vomit while they were unconscious. I doubted myself when my loved one was drunk because they got angry when I asked about it. I've rewritten the twelve steps into positive affirmations to resonate better with my loved ones.

I've been on suicide watch after depression took over, and I've sat in hospital rooms for weeks on end praying for my loved one's recovery. I've listened to my loved one's stories of abuse, but also of the abuse they witnessed as a child. I've nursed my loved one back to health as they learned to walk, bathe and feed themselves again. I've watched my loved one's body swell from liver failure to the size of a watermelon before draining the fluid. I've shaken loved ones silly, trying to wake them from blackouts. I've watched anguish and grief mentally break a child leading them to run away and I had to file a missing person's report.

I've lost friendships, my career, financial wellbeing, health, and intimate relationships. I've gained weight, lost hair, forgotten to eat or overate, developed PTSD and social anxiety, and had a mental breakdown. I've walked away for the sake of my mental health. I've stayed too long out of hope that the good times would return and we could be happy when they got sober. I've let my loved ones hit rock bottom alone, so they felt the impact and learned to self-correct. I've screamed, slammed doors, whipped wine glasses across the room, threatened, begged, suffered in silence, cried myself to sleep, ran for the hills, ignored, planted seeds, tried new angles— I did it all.

I witnessed and experienced addiction, but I instinctively saw deeper into the trauma and pain. I was woefully unprepared to handle most of what happened, and oh how my heart aches for it, but I did my best. In some cases, my best efforts saved someone's life, pulled them into treatment, and gave them room to heal. In others, my best removed children from harmful situations and saved them from some of the trauma they went through. And more than once, I could do nothing but let heartbreak wash over me.

Still, my own emotional, physical and mental wellbeing suffered. I escaped on trips for space, I experienced the worst panic attacks of my life, and in both cases, people suffered the consequences of my inability to cope. It isn't all that different from my loved ones' addictions. I just wasn't using substances to dull my pain.

So much confusion came from both the ability to understand my loved one's pain and suffering and the building resentment at not having my own needs met. But, of course, I wasn't asking for much. What I needed was the bare minimum of what one would expect in their intimate and family relationships. But addiction doesn't leave room for anyone else, and recovery focuses solely on The Addicted until family counseling and repair are involved.

Unfortunately, my relationship ended without that resolution—more than once. The last time was when my breakdown occurred. I spent hours on the kitchen floor, not being able to breathe with every emotion I held back for years, whipping me to shreds. There was no more denial, no refuge in hope. I didn't have an escape, and the reality was, it was all over. They were well, but they didn't need me anymore. My loved one didn't include me in their healing, whatever their reasoning, and my hopes were as shattered as my dreams. I was on my own.

Being needed, wanted, appreciated, and loved is a basic human need. But I put all my needs in someone else's hands, someone who wasn't healthy or capable enough to repair our relationship and work on sobriety simultaneously. Unfortunately, I wasn't healthy either. I had bottled years of unmet needs, pain, and frustration because I loved them and didn't want to worsen their drinking. Oh, I was honest with them and kept it real, but they never experienced the full range of my emotions. Now, there was no outlet for any of my feelings, good or bad, and I would never have my needs met— not by them.

I was finally, shockingly, heartbroken and cured of caretaking in one fell swoop!

It was where my healing truly began. Everything I was too busy to feel and process before showed up in waves, and I rode each one. I had never experienced such rage before. I wanted to do damage, show people that I was deserving of better, and make them give it to me. Intense feelings like that don't come with an instruction manual, and I did my best to soothe myself with gentle thoughts. However, a constant current of memories plagued my days which twisted into upsetting dreams at night. Talking about my feelings only upset me further, I'd retold those stories to death anyhow, so I learned to stop ruminating and let go. It took over a year, and I still catch myself getting lost in all the ways it should have been different at times.

However, allowing my feelings to ease gave me a bit more room to let in other things. My own goals and dreams started to form where I realized they didn't have anything to do with what my loved ones were doing. I focused on ME for the first time in my life. The more I adjusted my attention, the more peace I felt and the less scrutiny my loved ones experienced.

The less resentment I held, the more understanding I became and could love without any expectation. This thought process allowed the rewiring of my brain, so the hamster wheel disappeared. As a result, my relationships are healthier, and I can appreciate my loved ones as a whole person rather than the broken pieces needing fixing. Sure, I grieve for what I've lost, but there is room for growth and change now. Either old relationships evolve, or they fall away. My loved ones may be in recovery or addiction, but I can only participate within my boundaries and healthy choices. I know what healthy relationships involve and will accept nothing less.

I now know I cannot afford to.

I have a new resolve, a quiet one, a place in my heart that doesn't hold judgment or hatred even though it shattered into a million pieces. I wish I had never experienced addiction and how helpless it makes you feel. I wish I didn't witness physical ruin and death, but I did. I wish the panic and heartbreak didn't rob me of loving relationships, peace, and wellbeing over many years, but it did. But oh, am I glad to know what healing feels like and to feel calm again.

In the next chapter...

I will go into the lessons and revelations that resulted from my journey. You can't solve a problem until you know you have one and then understand its mechanisms. While the storm of addiction was unrelenting and painful, I began to see I had a power of my own.

Chapter Two

The Lessons

Addiction touched my life from many different angles. At times, it was indirectly present in the learned behaviors of children who grew up with alcoholic parents or in my peripheral vision of extended family; it was there but not part of my day-to-day life. At other times, addiction stripped me bare every day and ripped my desperate heart out with no reprieve in sight.

It didn't always show itself with obvious tells, and I questioned my logic over a subconscious need not to rock the boat. Addiction taught me not to trust myself because I didn't know the secret to stop it, and everything I did seemed wrong. The Addicted's unhealthy coping mechanisms trumped every need, want, or feeling I had. I was doing all the work to get my loved one back on track, and I exhausted myself in the effort.

"You can lead a horse to water, but you can't make them drink." I heard this many times over the years. I had shredded hands from pulling the rope, and no amount of kicking, screaming, or bribing got that damn horse any closer either. It took me years to give up and let the horse figure it out for itself.

Substance addiction is a life or death matter, but instead of an apparent wound that you can treat with first-aid or surgery, the underlying cause is deep-seated unresolved pain that kills people over time. Only, you don't know how much time you have left with them, whether stolen by an overdose or stretched out over years riddled with denial, excuses, manipulation, abuse, and slow decay of health.

I don't know which is worse, honestly. But, unfortunately, neither scenario leaves room for hope, and once that's gone, life becomes pretty devastating.

Of the four loved ones who struggled with addiction, three were with alcohol and one with drugs. None overdosed, but they were hospitalized on the cusp of death multiple times between the two of them.

Addiction doesn't follow any rules, and it is relentless. At one point, I was dealing with three of my loved ones' addictions simultaneously, and all three were in serious shape. The best I could do was manage whatever situation was in front of me at the time and move on to whatever the next responsibility was.

The strongest of us are often the most capable people, and without boundaries, the addicted learn to take advantage of our strengths. The more we take on and succeed, the less they need to show up and manage their own lives. As a result, we make life that much easier while we buckle under insurmountable pressure. It comes in the form of illness, mental breakdowns, anxiety, depression, weight issues, and strain on our work and other relationships.

The Aftermath

I had all of those issues. But, unfortunately, my final breakdown didn't come until after everyone was in recovery. I was so busy handling my kids, a business, my household, and the chaos of addiction that eighteen-hour days were regular with very little sleep. And when it finally calmed down, I was faced with the reality of what my life had become, where I had put my loyalty and faith, and I was grossly let down— primarily by me.

I felt unwanted, unloved, betrayed, unvalued, and a pure rage looking to inflict as much devastation as I experienced. My emotions were uncontrollable, and I couldn't find my grip on life. I can't say I was suicidal, but I couldn't see why anything was worth it anymore. My heart was finally shattered worse than ever in my life and, while it was a reprieve not to deal with addiction or struggles with sobriety, none of my needs were considered or put first and never would be. It was up to me now.

Who I thought I was, my morals and values— all incinerated. The most significant loss didn't turn out to be my relationships, my career, or financial security— it was the connection with myself.

Going out in public was painful and caused panic attacks. It was difficult seeing my family and friends because I couldn't tame my pain enough to be presentable. I felt like every word out of my mouth was raw vitriol not suitable for their ears. It would eventually get old anyhow. Plus, I didn't want my pain to upset them. I wouldn't say I liked feeling so vulnerable, and I lost all patience with my kids. However, they understood the pain I was in, which was very forgiving under the circumstances.

For the first time in my life, I only cared about myself. And it felt selfish and awful. I didn't know how to manage the conflicting feelings of not giving a shit about anyone and the loving, accepting person from before. I felt foreign to myself. Of course, I loved my kids, family, and friends, but my relationships had pulled me inside out and left me reeling. Addiction wasn't the problem after all. It was unresolved, deep-seated, raw pain that my loved ones couldn't face. I finally understood why someone would want to dive into a bottle or use drugs to obliterate reality. Reality fucking hurts, and I felt it without any anesthetic.

That kind of pain makes you writhe. But, then, fight, flight, freeze, or fawn instincts take control over rationality, and when escape is still not possible, numbing it out or facing it are the only options left. The fight response is to turn into the face of the threat and fight tooth and nail for survival. The flight response is to run as far and as fast from the threat as possible. The freeze response is to lose all sense of what to do when threatened and do nothing. Finally, the fawn response is to disappear and stay out of sight when faced with a threatening situation.

Thankfully, I chose to face it. I sat in my pain for months until I was too exhausted to care anymore. Pushing myself too fast made the pain worse, and while I knew I was working through depression, I went through the process without punishing myself over how long it was taking.

On my worst days, I replayed every horrible memory repeatedly in my mind. Internally I berated my loved one(s) for everything they put me through, especially walking out of our relationship and abandoning me again. I was frustrated with them for not being sober and showing up for their children. I hated that I was the 'bad guy' to everyone who didn't step in and help when they saw the risk. It was a constant loop that I couldn't escape even in my sleep.

On my best days, I refocused my attention on my pets or the weather outside. I found ways to take a mental break and forgive myself for not having it all together just yet. Hell, I'm still working on this.

All of my self-care practices had gone out the window, and the only routine I had was taking my kids to school, writing my book, and starting my business. I wasn't exercising like I wanted to, eating well, or meditating. I needed the mental distraction to take the edge off, overworking being my addiction, but I was slowly easing out of rage into resignation. Then, finally, maybe just enough healing to let go of it all for good.

The repeating cycle of memories is still there in my head. And just like addiction, my brain jumped to find the danger, be prepared and do everything in my power to avoid it. Except now, there was no one to worry about, and my brain was stuck in the circuit. But with time, the circuit loses the intensity of its charge, and there is room for other thoughts. My own goals and desires are more important than constantly catering to everyone else's. I see my closest friends again, take new adventures, and think about my future.

I have to admit, thinking about the future is scary. Through all the 'lifetimes' I already lived through, I had someone to worry about, take care of, plan with, and support me. Sure, addiction and imbalance were rampant, but there were a lot of happy memories, laughter, and joy too. Now with an empty nest before me, my life is becoming about what I want and need. Yes, any parent goes through this phase, and I saw it coming. But when I think about the level of hypervigilance and micromanaging I did to pull off the last fifteen years, it makes me feel like a newborn baby left to figure out the world all over again.

What I know now is that I have tools and practices to turn to, even when I'm out of shape or depression blurs the lines on me. I have learned a resiliency that nothing can take away from me. I'm learning to have faith in people again, though it's a steep learning curve to put down the old habit of hunting for problems and red flags. Surrounding myself with positive reinforcements taught me about attachment styles, codependent behaviors, and boundaries.

Life is one big lesson of experiences... good, bad, and everything in between. No one gets away with only a good life, and honestly, it would be boring and keep us from expanding into better, stronger people. Relationships are part of that ever-evolving mix, and just because someone suffers from addiction doesn't mean we don't love them deeply. However, we don't have to love their actions or the repercussions, nor do we have to take any crap from them.

It means that while I love you, I also love me, and my wellbeing is just as important as yours. If something is out of balance, dangerous, or unhealthy, I can't participate in it with you, no matter how badly I want to ease your pain. It means I see you, hear you and acknowledge your journey, but I can't join you on it unless it aligns with mine and in a direction where we can both be healthy and happy.

"Peace is the result of retraining your mind to process life as it is, rather than as you think it should be."
Dr. Wayne W. Dyer

The School of Addiction

My first lesson was about judgment. I was no different from many people who point their finger, think the answer is obvious, and mistake the substance or addictive behavior as the problem. I used a lot of 'well, they should' statements because I could see the damage very clearly.

It was back when I heard about the horrible accounts from my loved one's childhood. Not only was I a support person, but I was someone with answers. After all, I had experience with the assault center and providing resources for help. I'm good at being a shoulder to others' pain, but I shouldered the responsibility of putting plans and boundaries into place too. I managed without knowing about boundaries or what I was doing, and I found it confusing and conflicted. I made rules for people who should know better. It made me angry to be in that position, but worse, I was horrified for the children affected.

Not understanding addiction or the trauma behind it left me bitter towards The Addicted. I couldn't fathom how someone couldn't put their children first or see how bad their situation was. But this had been going on for years before I was ever in the picture, so I did my best to create a loving home where my loved ones could heal from childhood trauma and neglect. You know— lead by example. It doesn't work like that, though, and I blindly worked my butt off for my loved ones as their traumas played out in other heartbreaking ways.

My judgment disappeared beside a hospital bed. The Addicted was in total organ failure, and with only a few short hours to live and their body in ruins, I finally saw that no one would choose this for themselves. They couldn't manage life any other way, and it was gutwrenching to watch what it did to their children. In the end, I had nothing but love and respect for the person lying there, and I thanked the stars we had made it in time, so they weren't alone when they passed.

I learned that addiction is as much a physical reaction as it is mental and emotional. You can't just remove the substance, and voila! Everything is okay now. I discovered that addiction doesn't just touch the underbelly of society, but society treats people in addiction as if that's what they are. It's in homes you wouldn't even suspect and in families that appear to have it all together.

While addiction robs people of so much, I learned that it couldn't defeat love. The pain so many felt around their loved one's death was evidence of how greatly they loved them. Love lessens judgment, allowing understanding and compassion to return. Of course, it is difficult to love someone from any distance, especially when barraged with painful experiences, but space also provides perspective.

I stopped judging and started acknowledging that there was more than just alcoholism going on. I saw the soul who tried so hard but was finally at peace. And I saw the aftermath of grief, despair, and unresolved trauma that came afterward.

My second lesson was about compassion. I learned that too much empathy could be as dangerous as too little. I went from being a somewhat judgemental outsider to an intimate insider obsessed with preventing any more loved ones from dying. That meant protecting their kids, caretaking with meals, and shielding them from the stress of their responsibilities.

I learned that addiction doesn't make sense to anyone but the person in it. Even then, addiction sneaks up on a person, so they don't believe there is a problem until something dire happens. My intimate understanding of their pain made it easy to make excuses for their behavior or avoidance, which meant taking on way more than was my share and not allowing my loved ones to grow from their own mistakes.

I learned that you could endure a lot of pain and grief, but there is a point where a person breaks from it. It doesn't matter how good a person you are; your suffering can take over until your life is unrecognizable. My compassion gave my loved ones comfort and the chance to improve their lives, making addiction too comfortable without boundaries. The more trouble or denial they were in, the harder I tried, and the more desperate I felt. I was hard on myself, berating my actions every time I thought back on them until I realized that I deserved compassion too.

You can be understanding, loving, empathetic, and forgiving. Still, once you move from giving support to owning the outcome, you are now in codependence territory and lose focus on the bigger picture.

My third lesson was about standing my ground. I learned the reality of what the lack of boundaries will do and the difference between soft and hard boundaries.

Without boundaries, I couldn't say no to demands of my time and attention, which meant it became my perceived responsibility to solve all problems and needs that arose. As a result, I was exhausted but felt important and wanted.

Soft boundaries meant I had some idea of what I wanted and tried to implement rules or say no, but the difficulties it caused meant conflict or more work. So I would give up and let my loved ones get their way. It made me feel like I wasn't significant enough to be treated better. I was already too tired to add fights or the repeated nagging to the mix.

Hard boundaries were my absolute no. No more participating in the cycle, no more giving in, no more allowing my loved one's needs to supersede my own. When I said no, I meant it, and even though I had to explain my rules and expectations calmly, I wasn't willing to compromise on them. Hard boundaries were difficult, especially at first. I learned to hang up the phone even though it felt rude. I learned to explain my no once, then exit the conversation if not respected. I refused access to children unless my loved one was sober and working on recovery. I let my loved ones hit bottom and feel the full effects of their actions, including the severe consequences. I was only willing to help when they were actively taking steps to help themselves. Finally, I was so tired that I had no fight left to participate in anything that didn't serve the children or me.

In the end, my hard boundaries were where I saw the most improvement for myself and my loved ones. Of course, I wasn't perfect, and I'm still learning where my limits are. Sometimes the only way to stay firm on my boundary was to get mad or rude, but as I began to master this new skill, I found I wasn't getting as upset to stand my ground. By holding my boundary, I learned self-respect and how to love myself and my loved one more.

My fourth lesson was about true love. Love isn't just a feeling; it is an action. Love connects us and forms bonds that are essential for survival, comfort, procreation, and companionship.

I learned that love does not mean sacrificing yourself to save someone else when they are sinking in self-harming behaviors. It doesn't say, 'I am with you until the end, no matter what,' but rather, 'I love you and support you while you find your way.'

True love is loving someone without expectation, ultimatums, or demands for change. Unconditional love means that I see you, honor, and respect you at whatever stage of healing or happiness. I can do that in or outside of relationships and let go of the idea my happiness is contingent on theirs.

I discovered that where I made space for my loved ones' healing, I wasn't responsible for it— or conversely when they relapsed. As much as I loved them, it was okay to love myself too, and it didn't require deep sacrifice to be in a relationship. As much as they loved me, coping with their pain took all their energy, and they weren't capable of a healthy relationship while they were in active addiction.

True, unconditional love is just being loving, period. What is given freely is also received freely, and I don't want anything less for myself or my loved ones. I don't owe anyone love any more than they owe me, but I shut myself off from it for a long time. I learned that if you want love, you have to show up for it because avoiding people out of the fear of getting hurt also prevents you from being loved.

The only thing that could heal my mountain of hurt and loss was love because when I finally stopped ruminating in pain, I naturally came back into balance and felt love fill my heart once more. Love sees past the 'what' to discover the 'who and why.' It says that I am just as worthy of the tremendous love I gave away; therefore, I know what supports my growth and wellbeing and what does not.

I learned to love myself. It doesn't rely on anyone else to do it for me because I am enough as I am. And when others love me, they get the benefit of someone with an open heart.

My fifth lesson was about becoming selfish. Addiction seems so selfish because it takes over every waking moment for The Addicted and The Affected. Growing up, being selfish was unthinkable because my family always gave 100% of themselves. By my moral compass, it was the worst behavior there was. So setting boundaries, prioritizing my health and wellbeing, and reframing my caretaking mode fought one of my core values— hard!

I learned there is a big difference between destructive and constructive selfishness. But, I'm not going to lie; I wanted my loved ones to return the same level of love and devotion I had shown them. It only seemed fair! But this was immature of me because adult relationships don't work like that, especially in unhealthy dynamics.

Constructive selfishness is self-regulating instead of expecting someone else to soothe us. It's keeping to your own lane and focuses on what makes you happy without attaching your loved ones to the process. You allow yourself as much love, attention, reflection, and space as necessary for your healing without guilt or the need for excuses.

Destructive selfishness is where our actions cause people harm, intentional or not. It involves manipulation, lying, cheating, stealing, avoiding, abusing, controlling, and taking advantage of our loved ones. It is making decisions regardless of the consequences or the people getting hurt, even ourselves.

When I learned the difference, I could isolate areas where I felt guilt or resentment and recognize why I felt that way. Now, looking after myself and choosing my path didn't feel bad; it was a relief instead. I saw where my loved ones appeared selfish, and while it was true, it was a coping mechanism designed to prevent pain and trauma from surfacing. It had nothing to do with me, which was a significant revelation.

These lessons taught me where my codependent behaviors originated and why I held on so tightly in some cases and ran for the hills in others. As a result, I'm getting a better understanding of my relationship choices and what I'm willing, or not willing, to show up for. As a result, I have a gentle love for myself that I sought from other people before now, and I find it easier to forgive all my past choices.

I've learned to release my death grip so my memories aren't so painful, which allows me to appreciate my loved ones again. As I move forward with peace, they can too, and relationships can finally mend or fall away as a memory.

I continue to evaluate my feelings or where my responses are coming from, too. It is an ongoing process of self-discovery so that my old coping mechanisms aren't interfering with new relationships. The more I heal, the more I will trust myself and my future relationships without the shadow of my past hanging overhead.

I have learned that I am a mighty strong woman who endeavors to see the bigger picture, and when I can't, I step away to focus on myself rather than worry about others. There is great power in forgiveness, not because it excuses what others did, but because I'm no longer a prisoner of their actions. Forgiving gave me compassion for myself and the sense that the new Jenny isn't a replacement of the old but a freshly expanded, wiser version worthy of great love. People must earn a front-row seat to my show from now on or get relegated to the gallery.

Addiction has been one of the most monumental teachers of my life. It doesn't mean I deserved it, nor did my loved ones. I can't change how I handled certain situations, but thinking on it, maybe the wheels would've fallen off the bus entirely. Yet, on the other hand, perhaps we would have healed a lot sooner.

The point is that feeling guilty or shame is useless. It holds us captive to pain that won't resolve itself using the methods we've tried before. Shifting the energy with new tools and self-awareness allows the light to come in and breathe new life in a dark situation.

In the next chapter...

We look at addiction and codependency in greater depth and how we got stuck inside the storm of our loved ones' addiction.

Chapter Three

Addiction & Codependency

To be clear about addiction and codependency, they are coping mechanisms or behaviors that in no way define us as people. Unfortunately, society loves to slap labels on people, which are detrimental to getting help and healing. I don't endorse labels, and I encourage you to drop them as well.

Addiction is not rare or saved for bad people. Instead, it touches people's lives across every class, level of education, race, family structure, culture, and age group. Where there is trauma, there is pain; and without support, the trauma goes unrecognized, and the pain deepens.

Addiction is the result of a coping mechanism. The Affected are emotionally, mentally, and physically addicted to avoiding overwhelm from traumatic memories.

Addiction comes in the form of substance abuse with alcohol, drugs, cigarettes, and chewing tobacco. It is also in behaviors like gambling, sex, porn, eating disorders, exercise, and technology. Addiction can also be a combination of several substances and behaviors as one no longer does the trick. Addiction creates a reoccurring process revolving around triggers, cravings, seeking, satisfying, the void, and withdrawal— the more intense the addiction, the faster this cycle spins. Reality disappears, and maintaining a comfortable level of their cravings is their only focus. But there is never a comfortable level, and addiction takes them deeper, tricking them into feeling better.

Of course, family history, societal norms, pressures, or even cultural issues all play a significant factor in addiction, but we often focus on the result instead of the real problem.

It all stems from the pain of trauma. Pain from wanting to fit in and deciding to try drugs for the first time. Pain from being physically, mentally, or sexually abused or witnessing the abuse of others. Pain from heartache, embarrassment, shame, guilt, or lost love. Pain from illness or injury. Pain from a lost culture or identity that bleeds into generations. Pain that wasn't ours originally, but we learned our parent's coping mechanism to follow them into addiction. Pain from the loss of a job or business. Pain from their sexuality not being accepted by their family, peers, and society. Pain from the death of a loved one. Pain from being removed from family or kidnapping. Pain from feeling helpless, worthless, lost, depressed, or from mental illness.

Shall I go on?

Addiction is a multi-layered issue, unique to every person's story and yet the same at the very root— pain from trauma. They are IN PAIN. The less they can cope with their anguish, the farther in they go. Denial isn't just about their addiction, but also what happened in their lives or what they witnessed. If our loved one isn't ready to investigate the details of their past, then they are more likely to turn back to their coping method of choice.

Is it any wonder that we get caught up in the current of addiction with them? I certainly empathized with the enormity of what my loved ones were going through and only wanted the best for them. But, of course, the flip side was the need for their pain/addiction to end so that I wouldn't suffer anymore. It's damn uncomfortable to watch! We feel helpless! We are caught in the spokes as the wagon runs away with the horses.

What is worse is that our options are very limited to get that person help until they are willing.

Addiction is an illness that costs The Addicted and The Affected dearly. Within the circle of addiction lives codependency, which is no less devastating. The Affected suffer from diseases related to stress, car accidents due to lack of attention, suicide, depression, or forming their own addictions. Detaching from the emotional roller coaster is damn near impossible while strapped into the front of the ride. But that is the secret— detachment.

Let's define addiction based on what the dictionary tells us:

"The state of being enslaved to a habit or practice or something that is psychologically or physically habit-forming, as narcotics, to such an extent that its cessation causes severe trauma."

Wow— enslaved.

We can step back for a moment, consider the series of events that caused The Addicted's pain, and realize that this had nothing to do with us.

From a different viewpoint, we can see where they struggled and why they made the choices they did. Maybe now you can see that running away from the real problems was more manageable than facing them.

The trigger looks like this: Stress/pain/memories = anxiety = adrenaline = panic = self medicate/blow up/avoid

Until my loved ones went through treatment, recovery, and long-term sobriety, there was no chance of rewiring the biological response to liquor. And once they had accomplished that, they had to work hard at reprogramming denial. Then, finally, my loved ones had to learn when addictive responses were ringing their bells and put a self-care practice in place to counter them. We must do the same thing.

Now let's define codependency. Codependency, as an adjective, is described as:

"Of or relating to a relationship in which one person is physically or psychologically addicted, as to alcohol or gambling, and the other person is psychologically dependent on the first in an unhealthy way."

"One who is codependent or in a codependent relationship"

Essentially, this is saying that we are psychologically addicted to our relationship with The Addicted as it relates to keeping the peace, problem-solving, making excuses, masking the issue, and treading water to survive as The Affected.

This cycle is very similar to domestic abuse situations with a honeymoon period that transitions into tension until there is a blow-up and then peace for a short time. With addiction, the honeymoon period could be when they've agreed to get sober or appease you somehow, then gradually sobriety slips away until there is an undeniable event that causes chaos.

These cycles could be happening simultaneously, too; however, they will continue without breaking them with new behaviors and reactions.

It doesn't mean we don't have legitimate reasons for loving them or that we don't have wonderful memories together. But, it also doesn't make us bad people for trying to make a hopeless situation better somehow or silently wanting to kick them square in the ass. Addiction has a habit of saturating our memories until there is nothing left of happy times, and we can't look any longer. It is just too painful to watch. In resignation, our feelings can become harsh.

Let's take a moment here and consider our relationships right now. I want you to think of what your day looked like when your loved one was truly at their worst.

How many instances did you look for liquor bottles, check to see if their glass smelled of something other than pop, or their speech slurred? How much time did/do you spend compensating for their inability to manage their life? Do you take on responsibilities that aren't yours? Do you find yourself getting more and more obsessed with this routine? How much time a day do you spend thinking about their problem?

The closer you are to feeling obsessed over their addiction, the deeper into codependency you may be. If you think of addiction and codependency in terms of actions, the more frantic and erratic we are, the deeper in we are.

I say this with the utmost compassion because I was there too.

We simply aren't accomplishing anything other than running ourselves into the ground while making it easy for our loved ones to stay in their addiction.

I confess to constantly worrying about my loved ones because, quite frankly, their actions directly affected my daily work and home life. I couldn't go one hour without another problem or crisis popping up. I would get phone calls and texts all day long, sometimes from several loved ones. My main concern was whether one of my loved ones would jump off the deep end if I didn't tend to every demand or problem. Sleep was almost impossible because of the stress I was under.

Shall we add some firecrackers to the fire?

How many of your friends, relatives, and acquaintances made a point of asking you how your loved one is/was doing in hushed tones? Or told you some embarrassing story about what they saw or heard about them? And worse? The effing gossipers. Oh yes, they love to make things juicy out of our worst pain, don't they? But they also trigger every codependent behavior we have and send us running to check if anything they said was true.

The trigger looks like this: Stress/pain/memories = anxiety = adrenaline = panic = blow up/problem-solve/avoid

That happened to me plenty of times. I would find myself trying to work only to get pulled aside by a customer or employee, to hear all about what someone had said or witnessed about my loved one. The next thing I knew, I drove all over the city, checking on the situation. I would demand the truth, get into arguments and pretty much lose my mind at the lack of control I had over my loved one's behavior.

There can be genuinely kind people trying to show concern for you or your loved one, but for me, the previous experiences put me on high alert. As a result, I got highly defensive or unintentionally dismissive. I couldn't handle my loved one's addiction, never mind harmful gossip cornering me when I was already so overwhelmed. As a result, I pushed away from the very people who could be great supports and ended up even more alone.

It was a constant struggle for me. One minute I'm shutting my loved one down, refusing to listen to excuses about their drinking, and the next, I'm making my own so that I can hold my life together. I was more than aware of my loved one's denial about their situation. Still, I was less enchanted with the idea that I was also in denial.

Denial is the real ass-kicker of addiction and codependency. Remember, none of the repetitive, obsessive, and harmful actions of addiction and codependency define us as human beings. Instead, they are a part of our lives that need addressing so that we can get back to living. But denial will hold you back.

Denial

We don't see how our choices and behavior have resulted in our life circumstances, and the idea of taking responsibility is impossible for our fragile state of mind. Trauma and pain leave us looking for someone to be responsible, anyone but ourselves. Please don't misunderstand. I'm not excusing abuse or neglect but instead, refer to being stuck in the victim mode and not healing to become a survivor.

The Addicted choose to use substances or actions to numb out and avoid, while The Affected do the same. Denial leaves both making excuses to stay inside the cycle because, for one, they don't know any other way. For another, it is too scary and painful to change.

Our feelings are complex, and while valid, do not always serve our highest purpose. It is easier to be reactionary than pause and reflect on what is setting them off and self-correcting for a better outcome.

For The Affected, the cycle looks like this:

Trigger, anger, judgment, guilt, shame, blame, frustration, resignation, denial, trigger, anger, judgment, guilt, shame, blame, frustration and denial.

Are you beginning to see the cycle? Unfortunately, the hole we are digging just gets deeper and deeper. Something has to change to break the cycle.

As each emotion comes up and we project these feelings, The Addicted's response is to deny, get angry, avoid, appease, apologize, and then get their 'fix' as fast as possible.

As we experience their reactions and continued addiction, we add feelings of hope, relief, despair, fear, and resentment to create a roller coaster effect. The highs and lows are exhausting! The Affected then turn to coping mechanisms like food, cigarettes, shopping, sex, excuses, or other avoidance techniques. I've been there. I understand that anything feels better than dealing with addiction. But when the crutch is not available or no longer does the trick, our meltdown occurs.

We also project our feelings onto other people or events because we haven't acknowledged our real feelings. For example, my frustrations and emotional outbursts often came out by criticizing other drivers in traffic.

I would yell, "Somebody needs to teach these people how to drive!" I got explosive over minor irritations with my kids because I bottled my frustrations from the more severe issues around me.

Jenny Truth: The illness of addiction begins
with denial and starts to heal with its release.
The festering, gnawing, painful agony of
addiction can do nothing but grow, the grip
getting tighter and tighter until The Addicted is
no longer in denial or dies. I cannot determine
the right time to heal for anyone but myself.

It is not within my power to make someone wake up from their denial, even though it feels better when I stage an intervention or pour out the last of their liquor. It is only in my power to become aware of myself, where I then begin to solve my own problems. To eliminate addiction in my life, I must move past denial and retake command;

only then will I gain the strength to rebuild a life with joy and happiness.

So how do we know if we are in denial? See how these statements resonate with you.

1. My husband knows when to stop, and he has control of himself.

2. My child is just acting out in adolescence. Everyone goes through this.

3. I control the checkbook, so my wife can't spend the money on wine.

4. I'll let you back in one more time, but if this ever happens again....

5. He's only abusive when he's been drinking but is a good person when he is sober.

6. I've kept the lid on my wife's drinking problem from the kids. They have no idea.

7. It is out of control. I have no choice.

8. It will get better when dad quits doing drugs. Then I can be happy.

Ask yourself, do they make you uncomfortable? Do they sound too familiar? Do they make you angry or anxious? These are signs that all the excuses you have been telling yourself no longer hold water. I'm not judging you here. I'm merely offering a new way of looking at things. We take care of so many people, carrying far more than what is ours to bear, that we often don't consider what we need in life to be happy.

Even if you aren't in denial about the addiction, walking through some self-awareness steps is beneficial for finding healthier coping techniques. Be gentle with yourself as you answer, and write down your feelings as they come up. It begins with knowing where you're focused and why to give denial the first kick in the ass.

Settle in with your lovely journal, take some time out of your day where you won't have any interruptions, and answer honestly. Grab a box of tissue too. Expand on each question and journal how they make you feel. Pay close attention to any feelings of guilt or shame that come up and write about them too.

- **Are you focused on staying in the cycle, or are you focused on changing it? How?**
- **Whose life, relationship, or behavior am I trying to change?**
- **If it doesn't change, can I be happy? Why or why not?**
- **Is this my cycle or someone else's?**
- **How is this situation affecting my health?**
- **Is this within my power to change? Why or why not?**
- **If things don't change, then what?**
- **What am I truly scared of?**

The first time I started doing reflective work, I set myself up outside on my deck in the sunshine with a cup of tea and birds singing in the trees. With every question, I found that some difficult emotions started coming up, and I would stop. It was hard not to twitch, check my phone for messages, get up for more tea or do anything other than sit in that moment and just feel.

I let the feelings come, knowing that the Universe would only give me what I could handle at the time. So I wrote pages and pages with every ounce of hurt, rage, injustice, and fear I had until my hand cramped up. Then, when I needed to, I took a break.

The questions start picking at the scabs barely concealing your wounds. It is okay to allow it all to unfold at your own speed. Awareness is a new dawn and a powerful tool you will now use to your benefit. It will feel like losing twenty pounds of emotional crap. It is the realization that "Hey! I really can feel better!" Repeat this until you find yourself turning negative thoughts into something more positive. Focusing on happiness is your new habit instead of getting sunk into a rousing session of ruminating or 'stinking' thinking.'

These are the first steps to understanding your behaviors and maybe why you acted that way. Next is realizing who was responsible for what and how you lost track of that. These questions are keys to unlocking denial's defense mechanisms. Therefore, we need to pay close attention to feelings of shame or guilt. We have been busy little life-savers, and while we have been trying to manage the addiction in our lives, shame and guilt sneak into our subconscious.

It is okay! No matter what you experienced or what you wrote, that was your journey and your story to write. Remember to offer yourself compassion when you feel like tying yourself to the whipping post. You did the best you could under the circumstances with the tools you had available. Now you are finding new tools, so congratulate yourself for surviving it and use that experience to grow.

Read the following statements and see how you react. How does it feel when you hear them? Then, write the statements your loved one uses and describe your feelings about them in your journal. For example:

1. I haven't been drinking/doing drugs/gambling.

2. I am trying.

3. It's my life, and I can do what I want.

4. I am in complete control.

5. I can walk away (drinking/drugs/gambling) any time I want.

6. No one can tell that I have been drinking/doing drugs/ gambling.

7. One more isn't going to hurt.

8. Mom and Dad will always give me more money/a place to stay/ a ride.

9. You don't know what you are talking about.

10. If I stop cold turkey, it could be dangerous for me.

You may be all too familiar with their usual excuses, and it's evident that they are in denial about the mental, physical, emotional, and financial impact their addiction is having on you.

It can be hard to know the truth when The Addicted become master manipulators to keep us from upsetting the apple cart.

Like in my case, my loved ones learned a new set of healthy-sounding responses with every trip through rehabilitation. But they were still in denial about the extent of their addiction. The first three trips through the hospital and treatment centers didn't get deep enough, but my loved one learned something new from each one. I discovered that what sounded good in our open discussions about recovery and sobriety (what to avoid or not, what to talk about or not, what to ignore or not) was covering up an ongoing issue with guilt, shame, trauma, and denial. It was all hidden in the guise of what they learned in treatment. My loved one just wasn't ready to get to the root of the problem, and with the triggers still present at home, it proved too difficult a challenge.

It took a while for me to realize when the drinking started again. My loved one admitted to having a problem; therefore, not in denial about the issue— so I thought. But denial was present with the first drink, the sixth bottle, the tenth month, and the next detox and rehab. So around and around we went. My loved one's denial was rooted in thinking they had control and could stop anytime.

I was in denial because my hope for sobriety and repairing our lives superseded the writing on the wall. My loved one was working hard at hiding how much control the vodka had over them, and I couldn't face the idea of them losing the battle.

Denial kills people in and around addiction. Our denial can make addiction all too comfortable and a little too easy. Their addiction can turn us into battle-worn soldiers, hyper-alert to the next disaster until we too have PTSD, anxiety, and depression. We become elite spies, detecting our way through any red flags that addiction is returning or that we caught them in a lie.

It is all just so exhausting!

If we can move past denial for ourselves, then there is hope. Healthy choices and habits start to outweigh poor ones. We find ourselves on the path to physical, emotional, and mental wellbeing with newfound energy, one that begins to affect the rest of the household. Suddenly, we aren't waiting on them hand and foot, and our loved one begins to fend for themselves.

Again, without judgment, you get to decide what it looks like for you moving forward. It may mean that you recognize that it's time to change, but it may not be safe without a real plan. It may mean that leaving right now will cause serious financial woes. It may mean you are willing to set new boundaries and stick to them. It may mean nothing else changes about your loved one's life, but you have started doing some of the self-care techniques I mention in Chapter 7, and you suddenly discover the self-confidence you thought was long gone.

When Denial Lifts

Hitting the brick wall sucks. Nothing I did changed the addiction or any of the chaos it created. I burned myself out to the point of hysteria in a therapist's office one day, and I had nowhere to find answers. I couldn't tell if I was making the situation worse or helping my loved one. I had no clue.

I insisted on attending one of their addiction counseling sessions to find out.

"I don't know what to do anymore!" I cried. "I can't tell if I'm helping or making the situation worse!" I was a bawling mess.

The therapist took one look at me and said, "You need to consider getting counseling yourself." She said nothing more to me other than offer me a tissue. I was utterly exasperated by it. That was the last straw.

I was insulted, angry, frustrated, and aggravated.

All I could do was sit there and listen to the recommendation that my loved one check themselves into a detox and treatment facility. In my head, I was thinking, "Yes, but what about me?!" Instead of getting the answers I came for, they discussed my loved one's fear of getting help.

I was not calm or collected. I was not detached like the therapist was trained to be. I wasn't in denial, but now I felt lost and helpless about what I should or shouldn't be doing. And I still felt like I had to do SOMETHING.

So, what is the right thing to do? How do we regain the feeling of security and happiness when we can't get the drinking or drug use to stop? How do we face the very real possibility of their death?

Should we kick them out? Should we let them in? Should we call the police? Should we confront them? Should we pour out the liquor bottles? Should we move away? Should we get counseling? Should we put them in detox? Should I give them money? Should I change the locks? Should I give them a ride? Should I take them to an AA meeting? Should I refuse to talk to them? Should I ignore them? Should I hide what I did for them from my spouse? Should I get a divorce? Should I stay? Should I tell my family what is happening? Should I tell their family what is going on? Should I tell the kids? Should I lie? Should I tell the truth? Should I give up? Should I accept it? Should I forgive them? Should I punish them? Should I give them a book? Should I take responsibility? Should I give them more responsibility? Should I cancel my plans? Should I cater to them? Should I ask for help? Should I feel_____?

No wonder we are lost and confused!

We've all gone through these scenarios in our heads. We may have even done a few of them with varying success. We measure the pros and cons, knowing there would be fallout no matter what we do, so we chose to do nothing. It is less dramatic— yet still traumatic.

No doubt we've also been given all kinds of advice from friends and family who are not in the thick of it. Society and stigma have plenty to say about people lost in addiction, often without compassion. Of course, there are plenty of well-meaning people too, but all the advice just seems like a lost cause when every solution comes with enormous weight.

I had to start looking for my own answers. In the end, I was alone and had to choose what I allowed in my life. At that point, sitting in the therapist's office, I didn't think I had chosen a thing. It was all stuff that had happened to me. I could only find the answers by putting down my victim role and picking up a pen.

As I began to write about everything that happened, I became very aware of what I had been through.

I saw how my memory was affected because it was challenging to get my timeline straight. I saw just how much time had gone by— it felt like a thousand years ago and only yesterday simultaneously with big chunks of my memory missing. I realized how focused I was on misguided attempts to save my loved ones. I saw myself in the reflection for the first time, but I didn't recognize the woman staring back. I had lost touch with ME.

I started to see why I made certain decisions and how things could have played out differently by writing it out. Hindsight is only good if you are kind to yourself and ready to learn from it.

Let's get the past out of the way. When you are ready...

Write out your addiction story. Yes, the whole thing. Get messy, get ugly, be honest, and let all you have been hiding or holding in bleed out on the page. Finally, it is time to tell your story in your own words without worrying about anyone reading it. You've been silent long enough. So don't move on with the rest of the book just yet. Instead, make some sacred space and time for this journey where you can truly focus. Take your time, breathe, and write.

Congratulations! You have bravely released a past that taught you many valuable but painful lessons, and now you are ready to discover a new journey. Right this very moment, I want you to celebrate how powerful you are to have come so far. Forgive yourself for any negative feelings of judgment, shame, fear, guilt, or blame. It was a lesson in contrast so that you could begin changing in a more positive direction.

Next, we have to understand both ourselves and our loved ones in the present tense. Now that we have written about the past, we need to identify where we are today. It doesn't mean it's gone forever, but it lessens rumination on the past.

Again, write your responses to the following questions and elaborate on yes/no answers:

- Is The Addicted ready to hear what you have to say?
- Is The Addicted interested in getting better themselves?
- Are they in denial about their situation?
- How much is their addiction taking you away from what brings you joy in your life?
- Do you feel secure in having them in your home?
- Do you think you need to be there to hold down the fort so nothing terrible happens?
- Do you own any of the outcomes to their behavior?
- How much are your actions contributing to their addiction? Have you talked about the situation to anyone?

What comes next? You still want answers on what you should be doing.

The 'right thing to do' for who? The right thing for The Addicted will depend on their age and willingness to accept the offered help. The right thing may be to hold an intervention and let them decide their fate from there. The right thing may be to wait until the person is ready to hear you, but you set your boundaries firmly and refuse to budge. The right thing might be finding a safe compromise on your boundary without breaking it. The safe thing may be to let your loved one hit absolute rock bottom so they experience the enormity of their situation and seek help.

That is a tough one. But you need to know the truth.

"More addicts have died from soft landings than hitting rock bottom."

Counselor, Recovery Center

The more we save The Addicted, the longer they stay in addiction. Our loved ones remain in denial because someone will always protect them from the consequences of their decisions. As a result, they stay in denial, and the behavior continues.

The hardest thing I heard at the family retreat at the recovery center was that I was selfish to save them because I was more comfortable when they weren't suffering. Ooof! Gut punch. Yet, an undeniable truth. It was much easier to relieve my loved ones' suffering to ease my own.

The second most challenging thing I heard that weekend was that one in four of our loved ones would die of an overdose or related illness because of their addiction. There were easily eight to ten families in that room. I remember looking at these lovely people full of pain and desperation, wondering which of us was going to be left behind. It was a horrible reality, and they weren't wrong, as it turned out.

How much control do you need to have in the situation? If you let go, what will happen? If they run out of vodka, are you buying it to prevent abuse? If the bill doesn't get paid, then what? If they get arrested, are you covering it up? So what is YOURS to worry about, and what is THEIRS?

The right thing is to start defining this for yourself. You have complete control over what you experience in your life, believe it or not. You have more choice than you've allowed yourself, and your happiness and wellbeing need to be the priority.

What do you genuinely enjoy but end up putting off or canceling because your loved one wouldn't be comfortable? Are they not well enough for travel? Could they sell the cat or invade your home while you are away? Did you concede on your plans because it was simpler than following through and worrying the whole time?

If you have any kind of affirmative answer to those questions, then you know that you have put their addiction first, and it costs you too much.

The right thing to do is what gives you peace of mind inside your boundaries. It is what gives you security, laughter, and joy and soothes your soul. But it isn't easy. Breaking the cycle starts with just doing one thing differently.

Take a walk for the sake of fresh air. Bake your favorite kind of pie. Read a book. Say no when you mean it. Bring your focus to something that you can practice mindfulness on. If you can sing, then SING! Try that yoga or Pilate's class. Make your own Mala in a workshop. See the friends you have been missing and catch a funny movie.

The right thing to do is do YOU instead of treading water around THEM. The truth is, you can't do a damn thing for your loved ones until they are truly ready to do it for themselves. It is heartbreaking when we've done so much to support them.

Maybe it's time to leave the situation, or it's time to let them swim on their own and not come to the rescue. Maybe it's time to call them on their suicidal comments and call 911 for help. Or maybe it's packing you and the kids up in the middle of the night and staying at your sister's house. Maybe it isn't rocking the boat just yet.

Jenny Truth: You know when you are making the right decision when it feels better than not doing anything. When you don't feel quite the

same level of anxiety, fear, or gut-wrenching
stomach aches, that's the sign. It isn't the
easier decision, chosen out of lessening others'
pain.When one choice feels better over
another, that is your signal to follow that path.

You have imagined all the worst-case scenarios in your head anyhow. They could pitch a fit at you, break down the door, they could continue to struggle, and they could die. You are not at fault or to blame regardless of anyone else's feelings on the situation. You can't erase the trauma or pain they are in any more than you can remove the addiction.

Your job is to ensure you've got the basics covered, like food, shelter, and safety. Make mental health and self-care a priority. Get in touch with your inner child and learn what makes you laugh again. Get support when you need it.

Anonymous helplines can get you in touch with your local women's shelter, support services, offer advice, or just an ear. They will give you contact information for mental health resources. Reach out to support groups like Al-Anon, Facebook pages dedicated to helping people just like you, addiction counselors, and therapists. Talk to your most trusted friends or relatives and listen to what they have to say to you. I talk about this more in Chapter 8. Let some light in on what you have kept in the dark.

You may find it difficult at first, but that's okay. You may feel resistance to certain things, but start slow and see what fits. One day, you may feel differently about one support system or another. As you gain momentum and strength, your confidence will build. You will see there are lots of others just like you trying to live their lives despite addiction.

Judgment

Shedding light on our most painful experiences takes serious guts. Fear of being judged holds us back because someone could confirm our worst nightmares. They could think badly of us, and worse, our loved ones. But, if that happens, we can't deny the damage addiction has done.

On the other hand, we could reach out and discover compassion, understanding, and a new perspective that breaks the cycle of addiction and codependency. Instead, it cruelly robs people of trust and understanding, and it flat out sucks to be on the receiving end of judgment.

Almost weekly, someone would make a snide comment or attempt to get information about my loved one's problems. It made me incredibly defensive, protective, and downright mad.

Once, at a meeting, one guy went so far as to say, "They are a drunk and always have been." I could only stare at him in disbelief, and folks, I don't have a poker face. He could plainly see the pissed-off expression on my face. He shut up and carried on with his job.

Our fear of being labeled can hold us in unhealthy situations, including abuse, depression, mental illness, addiction, and debt. We don't want to admit our mistakes and have our dirty laundry flapping in the wind for all to see. We don't want to be embarrassed, gossiped about, or judged. Well, neither do our loved ones.

On one side of the coin, I dealt with grueling daily situations around addiction. It was like having one eye constantly drawn to the left while trying to focus on what was in front of me. My loved one's drinking pulled me in all kinds of directions.

On the other side, I handled questions and comments about their absences, whispered stories about sightings, and public gossip. Unfortunately, not many people were well-meaning, and I had to straighten them out more than once. It was bloody uncomfortable and embarrassing, and it caused me panic attacks every time. I was in a constant state of survival mode.

To have people make snide comments directly to your face about someone you love? And watch them walk away like they never had to wipe their own bum? Yeah, I didn't have very loving thoughts towards them at that moment. I don't give them much weight now, but at the time, it was devastating. I hadn't experienced many cruel people in my life until addiction was in the picture, and then, it was shocking.

The result was my loved one avoided people entirely, and I was a sitting duck. It also put me into overdrive protecting them. Eventually, I refused to talk to anyone who asked personal questions, and it got to the point where I couldn't handle the public at all.

Here are two definitions of judgment that I found particularly meaningful. The first:

"The forming of an opinion, estimate, notion, or conclusion, as from circumstances presented to the mind."

Based on our perception of a situation, our experience in life, and the ideals that hold true for us determine how we judge things. We then act on the idea or story we create in our heads after something happens from the circumstances presented to the mind.

Isn't it true that we use our personal experiences to form our interpretation of any and every situation we come across in life? Wouldn't it also be true that society teaches us to react within its norms? Either way, it is all reaction. Yet, rather than stepping back, considering the cause and effect of our actions, and choosing to act from our best selves, we jump with the crappy habit of judgment and, essentially, hurt many people.

The second:

"A misfortune regarded as inflicted by divine sentence, as for sin."

It puts a bad taste in my mouth when religion is used as an excuse for poor behavior. Tough love and boundaries are one thing, and they have an important place, but not as a moral advantage over someone else. I'm not saying that religious people are guilty of anything, but I take offense when church-going folk are cruel and use their attendance as some moral pass to behave badly.

Love each other. Be kind. Jesus was a healer— welcoming all. If we want to live in his example, we do not judge when someone is struggling. Instead, we offer our hand or a conversation, we allow them space to heal, and we are kind. If they aren't ready yet, we send them love anyway and let them choose their path. In an already difficult situation, does it add anything to be cruel or hurtful?

"There is always a positive way to say anything."

Doreen Virtue

Judgment isolates us from our human connection, gives us a swollen head and a shrunken heart. It removes our ability to relate, to understand, and to nourish not only ourselves but our neighbors, too.

I have found that I became less anxious and reactionary to stressful situations by pausing, and the outcomes were better. However, it is tricky because with all the drama/trauma we are experiencing with addiction, we are constantly reacting to something.

When I learned to catch myself in survival mode, I gave myself some time and space to think about what had set off my anxiety and then used my big girl words to explain what I felt or needed.

The only place for judgment is determining whether something feels good or not to our emotional guidance system. It is for your internal self-care practice to answer, "Is this good for me?" and then decide how YOU will act, not how you think someone else should behave.

The more we enter an experience with objectivity, pleasant or not, the less emotionally turbulent our lives are.

The difference for me now is I am past judging myself or anyone who taught me strength. People may judge me, but I will not participate in it. I don't hold hard feelings for the pain I experienced with my loved ones, yet there is no guarantee it won't return.

I have found that by releasing judgment, the path to healing becomes lighter.

Moving from Victim to Survivor

What is victimization?

We know what a victim is and that to 'victimize' is to 'make a victim' of someone.

How we act in this kind of victim mentality is entirely self-defeating. We get trapped in a negative holding pattern, never releasing the trauma out of fear that we will never be protected against it again. We are gripped in survival mode until one of our coping mechanisms kick in — healthy or not. The idea of being a victim shrinks our energy, whereas survivor expands it.

There is power in, "I am a survivor!" It says I have made it through the darkness and am still standing. I may have bruises, I may have a long journey of healing ahead of me, but dammit, I AM HERE!

And— you are finding your way to form new ways of thinking for yourself where you may have believed you were stuck before.

How does the role of the victim play out in addiction?

In truth, there are horrific stories of every kind out there with an incredible amount of unhealed trauma wounds to show for it.

"95-99% of people in addiction have experienced childhood trauma or loss."

Gabor Mate, M.D.

Holy shit! When I first heard this statistic, I almost fell out of my chair. It's horrible.

People cope with it in different ways. Sometimes, substance abuse or other addictions are the only coping tools they have. When our loved ones are stuck feeling helpless and weak, they fall to victim mode. Yet, when they find a glimmer of strength and self-esteem, they discover they are survivors.

So many have not sought help, attended group sessions or AA meetings to hear that they are not the only ones suffering. Emotional roller coasters take over their lives, and they experience ups and downs at lightning speed. Everything is terrifying, and happiness is a rare commodity. Without redirection, feelings of anger, resentment, shame, and self-inflicted flagellation are common. Addiction is just easier.

Our loved one's suffering is genuine. When it's quiet, we have more compassion. But when our loved ones use their pain to defend their addiction and behavior while taking it out on us?

Insert your response here.

I imagine compassion and empathy just hit the toilet, and you've given it a mighty flush.

The question is: Are you joining them in their victim role?

That's right. When your loved one is busy yelling, drinking, avoiding, excusing, demanding, and ignoring, are you reacting in equally useless ways? Are you stooping to their level, hoping you can get their attention to snap out of their thirty-five-year behavior pattern? Or are you backing up from the moment, recognizing it for what it is, and choosing to rise above?

In my experience, the longer my loved ones' addictions went on, the less tolerance I had. Any bullshit would set me off in a litany of honesty that could have cooked bacon. I wasn't buying what they were selling any longer, and I let them know it.

We were both stuck in the cycle.

The trouble was, it was doing severe damage to my health at the same time. I was touchy with everyone, my hair was falling out, my appetite was dwindling, and my ability to concentrate was gone. I would describe myself as 'scraggly with a flair for the dramatic' through this time in my life.

Thank the Universe for my mom and my close friends. They listened to me and kept my head in the reality zone. As a result, I found my way to meditation, energy healing, and some sanity.

But, honestly, I did feel helpless in my relationships. I felt wronged. I felt like everything I struggled to maintain had been for nothing. I felt like I was getting the short end of the stick. I felt like the victim of a catastrophic train wreck, not of my design.

What do we do when the whole world has fallen apart around us and no one comes to pull us out of the pit? We scream bloody murder at the Universe, at God, at anyone who isn't paying attention! Why is this happening to me? I don't deserve this! I deserve to be treated better! I deserve to be happy! It is bullshit! Who did this to me?!

And the sickening answer that I didn't want to admit? Yup. Me. I did it. I chose it. I own it. It was my lovely little crapload of stress, anxiety, anger, resentment, frustration, and blame. I was acting in full victim mode.

I say this with love, but honey, it has been you too. It seems like a ridiculous thing to admit, but we have found all the reasons under the sun to stay in the addiction storm with our loved ones— just like they have chosen not to get clean. We are in denial until we let go of the victim role and step forward as a mighty survivor with superhero strength.

It took my giving up altogether. It took me walking away and truly beginning to look at options for myself. It took me realizing what I was pulling off in my life without a single ounce of relying on anyone else for love, support, or sharing the load of a household.

I did it all and then some! Not only did I survive everything I was terrified of, but I also conquered it!

Getting past this stage is one that takes some honest reality checks, both in your behavior and that of your loved one. Awareness can happen in the blink of an eye, or it can take several baby steps with lots of practice. Finally, understand that no one can possibly be healthy when in the cycle of addiction and codependency.

It starts with understanding the difference between victim and survivor modes (different from survival mode). Next, it's recognizing which mode our loved one is operating in and then understanding it is not our role to fix them.

Victim Statements vs. Survivor Statements

Here are some examples of victim statements our loved ones may use so that you can see the difference:

1. My boss made me come to work when I told him I wasn't feeling well, and the roads are the shits! And now I've lost my phone, and I don't care anymore!

2. I don't want to drive, and I need to go to the store.

3. It's not my fault you didn't make the car payments! Where is all the money going?! You work full time. Why should I have to pay all the bills?!

4. It's no wonder I drink when no one leaves me the fuck alone! I'm fine, and I don't need anyone telling me what to do!

5. Here are some examples of victim statements we may use so that you can see the difference:

6. I can't believe Henry lost his cell phone in the snow and I have to look for it!

7. I have to drive Henry everywhere because he is always drinking. I can't risk him drinking and driving. It's not fair!

8. Henry blamed me for our car getting repossessed, but I am the one working all day while he sits on his ass at home. I'll have to get a second job!

9. I am going to leave you if you don't stop drinking! I've said it a thousand times!

10.

Notice how much caretaking also shows up here? In your journal, write down as many 'victim' statements you can recall making, including the way you were feeling at the time. Now here are some examples of survivor statements you and I may use:

I took a shower while Henry looked for his phone. He found it and went to work.

1. It is not my job to make it easier for Henry to get around after drinking.

2. I am not the only one responsible for our household. I am moving out to take control of my life, including my bills.

3. My empty threats haven't worked except to make me feel worse for staying. I need to evaluate my true feelings, prioritize my happiness, and act accordingly.

Now, write down all the times where you decided to let your loved one handle their mess. Include any feelings you have around this. Especially note if any guilt came up for you. Think back to when you ended up solving a problem that your loved one created for themselves. What do you do when your loved one is behaving like the victim? Are your responses and behaviors always the same?

Write down a list of all the ways you solve or take care of your loved one's issues that they should be able to complete themselves. Include how it made you feel. Then write a corresponding list of what you could have done differently.

Keep in mind this isn't about doing something else out of spite. We aren't stooping to act lesser than our highest self, merely finding a healthier solution.

Next, think back to the times you didn't cater to their victim mentality. Did anything change about their behavior or point of view? Write down all the examples you can think of and include how that made you feel.

Did you notice the difference? Do you feel a shift in tension, like you no longer carry the weight of responsibility?

Even if the shift is slight, there is an element of relief present when we recognize that we do have options in our actions. Sure, changing the comfort zone could cause some backlash, but just like taking the soother away from your toddler, you can expect a tantrum. However, it doesn't mean you have to change your decision. Instead, you can take a step back, evaluate what is for your highest good and move in that direction.

Your loved one is responsible for themselves, which may mean they fall flat on their face. But, I guarantee you, that may be what it takes to realize the changes they need to make for themselves. And if they are too deep to take the steps towards self-care, you may have to accept that.

Everyone has their path, and the goal is to be as healthy and happy as possible. However, it is not my job, nor even my right, to save my loved ones from their lessons. It may mean they get hurt; they may fail. It may mean they die. But, as soon as I released my idea of saving people, I freed myself from the slavery of addiction and codependency. I was no longer a victim.

Reflection

We just completed some major investigation on a prickly subject. We explored the realities of addiction and codependency in terms of our behaviors. We looked at how desperate we get for answers when our lives are upside down. A new perspective around judgment and victimization has perhaps brought a new awareness to old thought processes. Maybe this is what you have been thinking too, or maybe this was an astounding revelation you hadn't considered before. Either way, it was an experience in vulnerability.

Addiction has been gobbling up our happiness, focus, money, wellbeing, health, and love like Hungry Hippos eating marbles. Snap...snap...snap... they are all gone in the belly of the beast! It doesn't have any sugar coating on it! Extreme emotions surface that threaten to overwhelm us rather quickly by touching on these painfully delicate wounds. And with so many swirling around and busting loose, it can get tough to recognize which is which.

In the next chapter...

We walk through some of our reactions and feelings clouding the issue. We don't know how to make good decisions or think a situation through before reacting without understanding what emotions just got triggered. By examining our feelings and our habits around them, we get that much closer to not responding from an unhealthy mindset in codependent behaviors. The debris starts to slow, and we can see through the other side of the storm.

Awareness Affirmation

My life has been a series of lessons designed
just for me.
Where I thought I had been failing, I know now
that I was still learning.
I am a work in progress with infinite
possibilities.
With love, I release judgment of my past and
move forward with hope.
I am healing at my own pace and trust that all
will happen for me as it should.

Chapter Four

Emotion Awareness

When it comes to facing addiction, every emotion under the sun runs through our bodies. It can be good one minute and pure anguish the next after your good day runs smack into the wall of your loved one's addiction.

Every time I got a surprise phone call or odd-sounding text, my heart would jump. I experienced slurred conversations, rages, and threats of suicide. I've listened carefully to catch any sign of intoxication or dishonesty while my loved one tried to blow past my boundaries. And because I was so poor at maintaining boundaries initially, they often succeeded, causing me horrific panic attacks and an ongoing sense of dread. I never knew what was coming at me next, and on the days I was too worn out, I found myself yelling in frustration.

Addiction doesn't always leave room for good manners, consideration, empathy, or generosity. Either by The Addicted or The Affected.

Addiction has convinced the body that it needs alcohol (or substance of choice) and cannot survive without it. In the worst cases, it can't. When uncomfortable feelings arise, the niggle points them toward their fix instead of a healthy resolution. The quick fix soon grows into a binge, then days, weeks, and years of it. Addiction is never satisfied and is the growing hurricane that whips up our entire lives when it hits.

Our loved ones' trigger to feed the fix becomes our trigger to manage the chaos, the cyclone picking up speed until the momentum becomes out of control or something puts on the brakes. It may be recovery, us refusing to participate, or the death of one of us.

It doesn't take much to react when we are triggered, and, oh boy, do our loved ones know just where to whack our buttons the hardest. We go through so much, and we do it mostly alone. Short of saints and angels, everyone would lose their marbles at some point! Emotions feed off one another until someone loses their voice, hangs up the phone, or walks away.

That is until we learn to step back and recognize why we are reacting and to what. But, then, when we redirect it in less upsetting healthier ways, it is incredible how quickly our loved one realizes that something is different. We aren't spinning in the same direction as them anymore. Debris isn't flowing in the expected pattern. It gets uncomfortable, and they pause. And it is in that pause where glimmers of awareness are born.

Awareness brings a fresh perspective, a new opportunity for resolution, and maybe some peace of mind too— for everyone.

Our feelings are our internal guidance system trying to steer us in the direction of our intended path. When it feels wrong or off, we move to something that feels better. For The Addicted, addiction overrides our typical survival skills because the substance or behavior feels better. For The Affected, codependent fixing is less work than letting the shit hit the fan. Understanding that by keeping our calm and not stooping to losing our temper, we feel better and choose not to participate negatively.

As I began to handle my feelings and reactions better, I found answers that resonated with my goals. I saw how my anxiety began to dissipate, and I was more confident in my ability to handle my day-to-day life without losing my mind. It felt so good to feel the first hints at calmness again. I could finally breathe! I found some control in my life, and I simply couldn't bring myself to revert to my previous coping mechanisms.

The more I understood myself, the less shitty I felt, and my self-esteem began to rebuild. Until one day, forgiveness for myself arrived. Finally, I wasn't some crazy idiot running around with something to be ashamed of.

Instead, I could see how I was learning some tough lessons and whatever mistakes I had made, it wasn't worth holding the hurt any longer.

The idea of this chapter is to walk, step by step, through our most negative emotions until we begin to reach the ones that feel better. So keep rising and find your way to relief, happiness, and joy.

Fear

We will always hold a memory of our loved ones in our minds when they were sober, loving, kind, healthy, happy, and laughing. They are beautiful there. Their complexion looks robust, they have light in their eyes, and you remember the connection you had. Your loved one is whole, and nothing is wrong. We hold this image sacred in our hearts and return to it often. We carry the idea close of who our loved one is or would be without addiction.

Sometimes it's our only solace. And, it is also what sparks our greatest fears.

We love a person so dearly, seeing them differently in our minds. Then, when we open our eyes to find them in utter ruin, we experience enormous contrast, and it is shocking. Pain rips through our hearts, and the fear that we will never see them well again takes over. Hope sputters and coughs up fumes as we combat reality with our loving memories.

Maybe your loved one is your parent with a lifelong addiction, and you never knew them sober. Maybe your child, who was once so sweet and innocent, is now not only in addiction but participating in criminal activity to sustain their habit. Maybe your spouse has cheated on you, hurt you, or abandoned you and all you can do is stare at your wedding photo.

The pain is real. The fear is natural, and the loss is breathtakingly profound.

We have likely lived with these heartaches and fears for quite some time, even to the point of numbness. We probably don't even know that it's there, cooking away and waiting for the next trigger to set us off. And whoa! Is it spectacular when it does!

Fear can push us to do idiotic things. It can lead us to spy and tail our loved ones around town. It can make us enlist all our friends and family to tattle whenever their spying is successful. We can hurt ourselves in an attempt to get our loved one's attention and take us seriously. We speed in a frantic effort to catch our loved ones in the act of using or even prevent them from it. Who knows all the ways we have acted out of fear! WE JUST WANT THEM BACK!

Fear can even lead us to overcompensate with food, alcohol, pills, drugs, gambling, sex, exercise, overworking, or shopping. Do you have something excessive going on in your life? Yeah, fear has been messing with you, darling.

Fight, flight, freeze, or fawn— they are essential survival skills. But when we fight, we can get hurt, upset, dismissed, or worse, arrested. When we run for it, we substitute our unmet needs with the previously mentioned compensations. When we freeze, we don't eat, sleep, shower, or notice we're wearing the same clothes for three days. We can't concentrate, and depression sinks in. And when we fawn, we shrink down, hide, disappear, and stay out of sight. I've done them all, depending on the situation.

The fear of losing someone we love so much is the biggest fear I can think of. That is our immediate response when one of our friends or family gets a cancer diagnosis.

Oh my god, how bad is it? How much time do they have? What is the treatment? We are here for you with colored ribbons and GoFundMe accounts! We will get through this together!

That same fear grips us, but there is a stigma around addiction that changes the response to this life-threatening illness. It goes something like this.

Oh my god, what did you do to yourself? How could you do this? Don't you know that stuff will kill you? What will the neighbors, your boss, kids, parents, family, friends, or in-laws think? What do I do? I can't believe you would do this TO ME! I can't believe you did this TO YOURSELF! You need to get yourself cleaned up NOW. You can't come here, and you can't go there, you can't be seen like that! Why do you support them? How can you see them like that every day? You don't give them money! You can't be their support while they are still drinking/using/addicted. You should leave. I have no sympathy for someone who does this to themselves.

Cancer sees so much compassion and support, not just for the sick but also for their family. Everyone comes together in a loving tribe to do everything they can to keep the hope alive and see a recovery. Addiction sees so much isolation, judgment, labeling, and 'rules' that no one comes out feeling supported or hopeful. It just looks ugly and self-inflicted.

So, we may still have the same fear of losing our loved ones, but our reactions can be vastly different. It ranges from one of compassion and genuine concern to judgment, hysteria, and bad manners. As The Affected, we experience that same stigma and become afraid of the backlash whenever someone discovers 'the secret.' That fear can not only keep our loved ones from getting help but us too.

In a nutshell, fear is the limitation we place on ourselves when the idea of pain shows up.

It can keep us from loving someone, going on adventures, swimming with stingrays, or jumping from a waterfall. Instead of saving our lives from wild beasts, fear is just robbing us of our most significant opportunities to experience life and grow. With addiction, it keeps us from facing our pain and healing.

I think my fear met its match with my stubbornness. I just kept coming back to the ring with my boxing gloves up, ready to punch my way through the problems until I came out on top. Then, I would plow ahead because that was all I knew how to do and I was getting mighty beat up for it. Fear kept me in that ring, showing up fight after fight, insisting that this battle got played out until I won. And by winning, I mean that my loved one was in recovery and sober. It meant that I would hold the fort down and hold all the responsibility. It meant I would show everyone who doubted me that they were WRONG.

Kicking Fear's Ass

Let's look at how fear has been playing out in your life. Remember, we are releasing our grip on everything we have been trying to control. Fear has ruled your life long enough. It is safe to explore the garden where you planted all those seeds of doubt. The more we look, the more we will find the weeds and pull them out. You are planting a new garden now.

In your journal, write down your biggest fear(s). If it starts with your loved one in addiction, that's okay. If it begins with how your own life is playing out, that's fine too. Just write all your fear out on the pages and allow it to pass through you.

Next, answer the following:

- **What fears have held me back from my life?**
- **What would I do if I had no fear?**
- **Have I been operating in a fight, flight, freeze, or fawn mode?**
- **How has this mode affected my life?**
- **How has this mode affected my family and friends?**
- **How has my fear helped/hindered my loved one in addiction?**
- **When I am not scared, I feel_____**

When finished, take a moment here. Get up and do a wiggle dance, shake off the negative vibes, then place your hands on your heart with your eyes closed and smile. Just let some self-love in and feel the accomplishment of release. I'm not kidding— do it! It is the practice of saying, "Where I experienced fear before, I am now changing up my vibe to allow healing and positivity to take its place."

Moving away from fear allows us to begin processing other stuffed-down emotions. Fear kept them there, rooted deep in our gut. Those emotions start to come loose without it, and we don't need to hold on so tight. Nothing is as scary as staying stuck in the emotional muck and having no chance to change our lives. Without fear, we realize that it is okay to feel anything and everything that starts to bubble to the surface.

The first one is usually anger. We aren't running in flight mode anymore, but our instincts are still in full gear. We aren't in freeze mode because we decided to read (and write) this book and begin moving again. We have gone through hell, and our nerves are jumpy. We don't want this to affect us anymore. We are willing to stand up for ourselves, and we are serious about it.

Moving through anger is the next step.

Anger

It is easily the first feeling that comes up when we are smack in the middle of a crisis with our loved one. We find an empty bottle, there is a mess all over the living room, the kids not picked up from school, or our loved one can't remember what happened yesterday. How is this even possible they can't see what this is doing to their lives? How can they do this to me!

Don't deny it. Even while you quietly put the bottle in the recycling bin and clean up the living room, you are fuming inside. You've gotten too good at stuffing it all down.

I'll push it right down into the depths of my gut, and then I'll eat my way out of my feelings later!

We hold our tongue, knowing that a confrontation at this point is useless. We will just get some drunken reply that pisses us off more. Maybe we will try to discuss it when our loved one is sober or in a better mood. Perhaps this has happened so much we don't bother saying, "I am not your maid, and you get to clean up your pigsty."

Then there are the more critical and irresponsible events where there is no holding your anger back, like forgetting the children, for example. That usually has a more immediate reaction, and it comes with an extra kick of motherly/fatherly protective instinct. So look out because I might actually rip you a new asshole this time! Good luck ignoring me now!

Unresolved anger is scary for a couple of reasons.

Our body reacts to emotions right down into every cell, and when we are literally vibrating with anger or rage, that vibration carries out in our physical health. It makes us sick with our cells now fighting each other rather than cooperating. We get triggered into a fight or flight response, but we are not doing either, resulting in internal conflict rather than external release. The Universe likes to find other ways to get your anger out, so you may start manifesting things like rude customers, car accidents, or your kid stealing your debit card for late-night Slurpees. Here, if you won't get mad about that, I'll give you something to get mad about!

Secondly, that fight/flight response is now playing out in your work life, your relationships with friends and family, and your ability to cope. You can't handle the person who just cut you off in traffic. You lost your cool on a customer at work. You got so distracted by all the inner dialogue that now you are the one who forgot to pick the kids up from school. The anger turns us into walking grenades looking for the first person willing to pull that pin. Unresolved anger leads to resentment and a lot of negative self-talk.

I had such a hard time around this. My need for good manners and being polite was crossing hairs with my need to get away. I hate being rude, but I was not in any shape to handle myself with grace. I had no escape from the storm, stress, or responsibilities, and I had to get over my feelings so fast in the public eye that I never had a chance to process them or react better. It seemed like I was taking blow after blow with no end in sight.

My anger came out by yelling at my kids and pets, throwing things, storming in, storming out, slamming doors, or even driving way too fast. I was defensive all the time, impatient and insistent. I was raving mad. I pretended politeness and professionalism when all I wanted to do was scream and run away.

I cried— a lot. Angry tears would frustrate me even more as I tried to stay as calm as possible. I felt worse every time I lost control and usually had to apologize to someone for it. Anger and rage were very uncomfortable for me and, until I found the choice of taking space for myself, they took over.

It starts with awareness. Complete this exercise and write your responses in your journal:

- I feel angry when he/she _____.
- I react by _____.
- When he/she ignores me, I feel _____.
- I react by _____.
- When I get angry I _____.
- How often do I get angry?
- How do I feel about myself when I get angry?
- What will happen if I don't do anything?
- What can you do to handle this situation in a healthy way?

You may not have all the answers on how to handle your anger just yet. That's okay. You took your first steps to understand how anger has been playing out in your life. Anger is a natural response to some of the crap we have dealt with, but more happens when it becomes a habit. By examining your reactions, you can see some of your patterns and how the fallout affects the situation. You then get the chance to see the cycle for what it is and how anger is limiting you.

When I found another way to express my feelings without reacting to every upsetting thing, I found my first taste of detachment. We go over that more in Chapter 5, but it was like seeing the scene from a fresh pair of eyes. My new reaction made my loved ones realize I was unwilling to interact if they were blowing up, using, or disrespecting my boundaries.

The less we fed off each other's emotional upsets, the more we could properly communicate. So they began to happen less often, and when it started to head down that road, we recognized it and ended the conversation before it got worse.

The truth is, some terrible things happen within addiction. Just seeing your parent, spouse, mother, father, or child lost in a haze of intoxication is something we never forget. They are the walking dead some days, and it's terrifying. We find ways to protect ourselves, and that anger can carry forward for years, affecting us so psychologically that we never get well. It can sour the best of relationships and make us prone to repeating the cycle of abuse and addiction.

The feeling of anger is telling us, with great might and immediate attention, something isn't right. Whatever is happening is going against our need to feel safe and our ability to trust. Examining our anger and understanding that we have control over our choices gives us back the power that we lost in our loved one's decisions in addiction.

Anger is an explosive response that comes from our fight mode. The first burst of anger is short-lived, but it can stew under the skin for a while. Once the excitement and drama/trauma wear off, other thoughts start getting our attention. We may think a little clearer now that the sparks aren't flying, but the anger will continue to resonate unless we resolve it. Then, anger will fester and turn into resentment, or it will be released.

Resentment & Blame

From the hurt side of us, it is easy to point the finger directly at the problem and its source. But, you can't fool me. You didn't want to clean up a month's worth of rotting food after your loved one left for treatment. You didn't want to pay your loved one's rent for the third time. You didn't want to start all over again, raising children that aren't yours. You didn't want to watch them wither away and die in front of you. You didn't want to have to bury them. You didn't ask for this. You didn't think this would ever happen to you... or them. Me either, honey.

Our happiness doesn't even seem to matter. The chaos is going on as our loved ones only focus on getting their next fix.

I struggled to hold down my household, three kids in school, bills, mental health disorders, the hospital, doctors, my mental health, a loved one dealing with alcohol abuse, another with drugs, the death of a third and the fourth in and out of treatment with death knocking at the door. There was no time for me to go to a gym, massage, golfing, or see my friends. Self-care was almost nonexistent. Damn right, I resented being put in that position! Damn right, I wanted something different for myself!

I needed my job. I needed my love to matter to someone. I needed my children to be safe and happy. I needed my loved ones to be safe and happy too.

I resented that I was more than capable of handling everything when more and more responsibilities showed up for me to do. I resented my loved ones for their denial and lack of compassion, not seeing what their addiction was doing to me. I resented being the only one willing to do anything to finally get a mental health diagnosis for one of them and the gauntlet I endured to achieve it. I resented being the only one with a license to drive my kids around after a loved one lost theirs to drunk driving. Finally, I resented being asked for money while I struggled to pay my bills.

Somehow through it all, I kept telling my truth. I didn't hide my feelings or say, "Oh, yes. Let me get right on that for you." Nope. I fought back, I challenged, I disagreed, and I refused. While forced to make do with the situation I found myself in, I was also unwilling to accept any crap from anyone. I wasn't blindly following along.

The difficulty I had was realizing I had the power to change my life. I was too scared of what would happen to me if I made significant life changes. They were too big for me to handle then, and I stayed put in my comfort zone— even though it was brutal.

Resentment and blame are the next steps past anger, but they are easy places to get stuck, and those low vibrational emotions don't make way for empowerment. It's not healthy to feel bitter when these uncomfortable circumstances happen to you. Understandably, you would blame The Addicted for creating such a mess. Yet, if we step outside of our feelings for a moment, we know that addiction is an illness that we treat differently than, say, cancer or stroke. Those same diseases can have the same outcomes that you resented earlier, but you have far more compassion for a person who has cancer, had a stroke, or is battling dementia. We go through resentment and blame with those illnesses, too; only the feelings don't last as long.

With addiction, we tend to hold onto resentment and blame way longer, and really, it's hurting us. But, unfortunately, we hurt the other people who are involved too.

For example:

A mother and father have watched their daughter struggle with drug addiction for the last five years. The mother has a better understanding of the struggles or the deeper issues of their daughter's addiction and the underlying issues than the father. Yet, the latter feels bitter about the whole situation.

The father takes his frustrations out on the mother, and his resentment builds until their relationship is on the brink of divorce. Then he blames his daughter for the marriage problems they are having.

By not recognizing these feelings, resentment festers and prevents us from moving on. Instead, we slip backward to anger and fear. We think that we know where the problem lies, and we know for sure who to blame, but that's just keeping us trapped right where we are. We are now enabling our pain, possibly growing an unhealthy environment for ourselves and our loved ones in addiction. So round and round we go, still caught in the cog.

Ask yourself these questions and journal the answers:

- **What do I resent the most?**
- **How is resentment affecting my life?**

- **How long have I felt this way?**
- **How does resentment make me feel?**
- **If I released my resentment, what would happen?**

By stepping outside of our emotions, we can see that resentment isn't getting us anywhere. This self-righteous bitterness makes us certain we are right all the time. We get a bit of an ego going that justifies everything we say and do. No one wants to be around you. You are sarcastic and miserable, biting off anyone's head who dares oppose your way of thinking. It isn't pretty.

Recognizing our bitterness and then releasing it allows us to grow towards compassion and understanding. Seeing that we did the best we could help to develop our confidence to do our best again. Doing our best encourages our loved ones to improve too. Behaving poorly just generates more of the same. Staying attached to wrongdoings is robbing you of much-deserved peace.

Looking back, I discovered my true strength in who I AM. I can do anything, no matter what, and I don't need to rely on anyone. I broke the unhealthy habits I formed, and I could clearly see what I wanted in my life. If I were to continue resenting the situation, I would be robbing myself of my newfound confidence. I would likely stay stuck in codependent behaviors, and it would likely push my loved ones into a corner until they began drinking again. In addition, my blame game could have resulted in shame, which can be a contributing trigger for someone in recovery. I actively focused on my feelings until my loved ones were well enough and willing to focus on the issues together.

Honestly, processing our feelings is complicated, especially when we don't feel great about what we have said or done. Our steps towards a new healthy outlook don't come without their growing pains either. We must have courage and trust that we are on the path. It is leading us in the right direction.

When we understand the impact of resentment, we naturally could shift into feeling guilt or even shame. It isn't precisely 'leveling up' on the vibration scale, if you know what I mean. Shame and guilt are uncomfortable, yes. We avoid those feelings at all costs, and they likely landed us in hot water in the past. But we must process these difficult feelings to begin turning towards a loving belief of ourselves. That is how we start to feel the progress that we are making.

Guilt

Guilt and shame are some of the most uncomfortable experiences we go through, with a lot of confusion tied in for good measure. As a child, I quickly learned that getting into trouble came with many tumultuous feelings directed my way. It completely bombarded me with displeasure from people I loved. Two things came from this: I either learned to cover up what I was doing wrong or avoided trouble altogether. I would do anything to avoid getting into trouble because the result was devastating to me.

Yes, I became the goody-goody child. I didn't party. I didn't do drugs. I drank rum at a friend's house a few times after sneaking it from her parent's liquor cabinet. I studied, wrote all kinds of bits and bobs about who knows what, and read books— a lot. My parents were more likely concerned about my heartbreaks than me getting into any trouble.

Fast forward twenty-five years, and here we are discussing some pretty deep subjects. First, I know that I am empathic, and I feel the other person's pain and want to fix it. Second, I want to make people happy. Yup— that fits. I feel the urge to help, heal, solve, salve, or remove any burden I can.

Of course, some unresolved childhood attachment styles, etc., are likely playing their part, but that is another book for another day.

So, when I wasn't successful at making people feel better, I felt extreme guilt. I felt like I wasn't good enough and failed my loved ones in the situation. The closer to guilt I got, the more upset I became until I was angry.

See how easy it is to slide?

When I was at the hospital with my loved ones, I had the time to question my part in the situation. I knew I had no control over what they were doing, but it picked at me that there were times that I didn't have compassion, patience, or even love. I don't have room for hate in my life, but I know that I judged and blamed them for their issues landing in my lap. The natural evolution of these feelings leads to guilt, then shame.

Heck, we get questions from caring or nosy well-meaning (or not so well-meaning) people. We get put in the position to either tell the truth, which whips up a hornet's nest of its own, or to lie. Lying about it builds anxiety, stress, anguish, despair.... then you guessed it more guilt and shame.

I got so angry for being put in that position that I finally started saying to people, "They make their own decisions, and it isn't appropriate to discuss their lives or choices." When I confronted them on their inappropriate questioning, people became taken aback, but that wasn't my problem. I didn't appreciate being the bad guy or the one to set them straight. I reprimanded people on more than one occasion. It was awful.

Unknowingly, they had put me in the caretaking position, like it was my responsibility to inform everyone about my loved one's whereabouts or actions. I resented it. But I also didn't like being rude, and guilt would take over. Eventually, I got better at handling myself, and it helped to realize that if any of these people were genuinely interested in my loved one, they could call in person rather than ask me. It simply wasn't my place to discuss it. I knew they were looking to 'spread the word,' and I wasn't willing to play their gossip games.

My experience with guilt didn't stop there. Before I gained my chops in self-care, I felt guilty for not calling in the troops sooner, for the level of destruction my loved one reached, for feeling helpless, and for causing hurt when I was about to deliver news that would devastate a family. I felt guilty for getting angry, for dismissing various signs I knew were trouble. But, worse, I felt guilty for any feeling that seemed to go against the grain of my naturally caring self.

I don't carry this around with me now, but I know I've walked through some dark places, grumbling some unkind words to myself about The Addicted in my life.

Guilt hits us when we soothed the beast and bought the bottle for them or brought over the drinks on holidays. It's waiting around the corner after we've made yet one more excuse to the children when their mother can't attend their Christmas concert or baseball game. It's ready to stab us in the heart when we wish for anything or anyone that would be healthier or better for us in our lives. This heavy emotion is right there, sitting on our chest when we realize how much time we devoted to all this chaos.

Get out your journal and answer the following:

- **What do I feel guilty for?**
- **Who has made me feel guilty, and why?**
- **When I feel guilty, I react by_____?**
- **How has guilt held me back in my life?**
- **If I choose not to feel guilt anymore, what would happen?**
- **How would I feel if I released guilt in my life?**

It is difficult not to feel guilty for feeling guilty, hey? But the questions are not designed to make you feel bad. These questions are your journey to an awareness you never had before. Be grateful for what you are learning about yourself. These careful steps are reflections only, and you are now building a six-pack of self-care muscles.

Guilt is the emotion that stunts forgiveness. It is the 'you have to feel bad because we say so' feeling. Guilt becomes so uncomfortable that it needs to evolve. Depending on how healthy our outlook is, it becomes a life lesson, or it morphs through phases of humiliation, self-reproach, chastising, grief, and internal flogging. In short, we beat ourselves into a pulp over it. When released, we recognize our lessons through our journey and feel stronger for it. But when we continue to bathe in guilt, the water gets murky with shame.

Shame

If guilt is our initial reaction, then shame is what we create through our negative thinking around guilt. Can you feel guilt without also experiencing shame? To my way of thinking, no.

When shame lingers, it becomes the element that burns away our self-worth, our confidence whittles down, and our inner child cringes at how small we feel. It can get so uncomfortable that we begin to compensate with self-harm to alleviate the internal conflict.

In this way, I can also see how shame engulfs a person into a raging addiction. Judgment and shame, in my opinion, are the root of unhealed trauma. Humans can endure pain, loss, embarrassment, and confusion from a traumatic event, but when they feel humiliation, shame, or judgment because of it, that is where the deep wounds fester.

Those struggling, whether it be with addiction, depression, or mental health issues, feel pain so intensely that they believe they cannot escape. Their reality does not change, and they are harder on themselves than anyone can imagine. I have witnessed this. I have suffered while watching it. I did what I could to restore a little self-worth so my loved ones could lift their heads and see themselves in a different light. A little kindness can bring about a little hope, then a slight smile, and maybe even the motivation to believe there can be another way.

'Planting a Seed' is a term I have heard time and again. It is the act of offering an idea to a person, watering it a little, giving it some sunshine, and seeing what grows from it. It isn't about owning the outcome but rather seeing if it found the right environment and timing to flourish. As a result, that seed has a better chance of taking root in kindness and love than it does in acid.

Let's plant a seed right now.

Write out the following affirmation in your journal:

I am a student in life. I know that I am always learning with the goal of spiritual, emotional, and physical growth. I know that I learn by falling, the unfamiliar, the uncomfortable, and trying new things. The outcome is unknown. I know that as I understand, I discover what feels good and what doesn't, constantly moving back towards what feels better for me. I know that when I do that, I am doing my best and following my intuition. When I see that I am doing everything I can for the best possible outcome, I know that I have also been doing my best throughout my life. I forgive myself for learning things ungracefully through a more challenging course than I expected. I forgive myself for learning it the hard way, but I am grateful for learning the lesson anyway. I am thankful for where I am on this journey right now, and I trust that I will see myself through anything that comes along. I see now that guilt and shame aren't necessary for me to learn my lessons. I see that feeling bad is not necessary and only temporary, and I release it. I am healing and recognize those who are trying to heal too. I see my path is for me as their path is for them, and I am free to choose how I feel, what I experience, and what I create every day.

Once you have written this statement out, re-read it. Let the words soak into your heart, feeling the difference of relief. Does your heart feel lighter? Do you feel a sense of release? Allow yourself a few minutes to absorb it all, and then write out how you feel now.

Now write the following underneath.

I am forgiven. I am loved. I am learning. I am Light. I am Blessed. I am Strong. I am supported. I am Free.

Sometimes people think they need to wait for permission to be free of guilt or shame, and someone's forgiveness must be the only way to redemption. Please don't wait for 'I forgive you' to move past the storm you have raging around in your head. Let go of the idea that someone else holds the magic wand capable of making it better. The people who tend to be the most judgmental also tend to be unable to forgive anyhow. Let them sit in their own 'stinky soup' and walk away, knowing you've just gained some serious emotional clout for yourself.

It is also in you to forgive those who have hurt you. You no longer need to carry the burden with you. You can let go now.

Forgiveness

Let's face it. Forgiveness is a tricky little bugger! It peaks around the corner, looking kind of cute with big doe eyes, and we sneak towards it, hoping not to scare it off. Then, just as we think we have convinced it to come out from its hiding place, a flash of memory strikes, startling us and POOF! Forgiveness has eluded us again.

There are two elements to forgiveness. First, it can feel like a double-edged sword, and second, the quiet relief after the storm.

It is twofold, the forgiveness of others and forgiveness of ourselves.

It is easy for me to pull up all kinds of hurtful memories that engulf me. I'm sure you can think of many infractions, both recent and in the past, that were the cause of distress and heartbreak too. It doesn't just happen with addiction or abuse; it is an everyday occurrence and a very human experience. There is an antagonist and protagonist in our story. Depending on the enormity of what happened, we either held on to every detail, including the damage it did, or we let it go and didn't give much more thought. We base our ability to trust on how many times we were hurt or let down.

Everyone in our life lets us down; let's be honest. But I would reason to say that most of the people in our lives didn't intend to and would be remorseful about it. For those of you who ended up surrounded by indifferent people, I hope that you know that you don't have to continue allowing those people in your life. Forgiveness came quickly when your husband forgot to buy mouthwash at the store and less so when they forgot groceries altogether because they stopped at the liquor store. There are worse examples I could hash out here, but I know that all of us can insert any number of scenarios that we would find more challenging to forgive.

The idea of forgiving someone for doing something so malicious, hateful, terrorizing, abusive, harmful, inappropriate, rude, dishonest, and shocking is somewhat tricky. The idea of forgiving the real villains in our story makes us squirm. We shouldn't forgive because then we make excuses for this behavior, and we would somehow be guilty too. And we will do anything to avoid feeling guilty, right?

I think we get mixed up in a lot of poor thinking when we allow 'the mob' to dictate our feelings or actions based on 'shoulds.' That's a trap into becoming a sheep, following rather than stepping forward in free thought.

It's damn uncomfortable to contemplate forgiveness. But, I commend suffering people who find the bravery to forgive. Not because it makes them look good, but because cutting themselves off from peace, love, hope, and healing is just not something they can bear to do to themselves anymore.

There is a quote about forgiveness that speaks to this.

"When a deep injury is done to us, we never heal until we forgive."

Nelson Mandela

Not to forgive is to carry the suffering with us through our lives, sullying our livelihood, families, health, and heart. But it's so effing heavy!

It isn't about allowing or permitting any of the behaviors around these incidents, either. It is simply not allowing the wound to stay fresh by ripping it open every day with a fresh round of ruminating. Everyone has a different process and timeline to get there, if they can manage it at all. It isn't my right to tell anyone how to process their grief, pain, or anger. I'm just suggesting that we process it to get back to living our lives the best way we know how.

I still feel the hurt from time to time when I remember how it felt to lose a child after being kidnapped. It was a horrible thing to do to people you are supposed to love and support. I can dig myself right into indignation, getting angrier by the second, until I'm pissed off all over again. Or, I allow that to be something I can not change and be grateful that the same kid grew up to be happy in their life and hopefully leave some of the pain of their childhood behind. I finally let go of my resentment and blessed it for the best possible outcome.

The act of forgiveness doesn't have to be face-to-face or involve the offending person at all. It can be sitting on a rock in the mountains in a private conversation with the Universe. You can make it a little ceremony with a candle and a prayer.

It can be an affirmation like:

I am walking my path through my feelings. I am allowing the time for healing to take place, however long that may be. I am okay if it takes me a while to reach forgiveness. I am worthy of giving and receiving forgiveness when I am ready.

When we have carried guilt and shame around for some time, it can be challenging to forgive ourselves. We have hurt people out there. None of us get to escape that reality either. I guarantee you that our loved ones are fully aware of how their addictions have impacted us.

It takes guts to apologize, especially first. Not getting an apology can hold us in a pattern of anger and resentment, so it may be more worthwhile to give your emotions some time to cool off then discuss them with the other person to come to a mutual understanding. You may get one (give one), or you may not.

Move through the following questions and see what comes up for you. Then, writing your answers in your journal, ask yourself:

- **If I forgive them, how will I feel?**

- If I don't forgive them, how will I feel?
- If they forgive me, how will I feel?
- If they don't forgive me, how will I feel?
- Are they waiting for me to forgive them before they can find forgiveness for themselves?
- Am I waiting for them to forgive me before I can find forgiveness for myself?
- How far away from forgiveness am I?
- What would it take for me to forgive them?
- What do I need to find forgiveness for?
- Why am I not ready?
- Why am I ready?
- What happens if I do not forgive them?
- What happens if they do not forgive me?

The paradox is that without forgiveness, the hurt continues not just for you but also for your loved one. Both of you will carry it around and use it as a righteous weapon against each other whenever life starts to resemble the original infraction. It holds us in a state of fear, subconsciously waiting for the subsequent offense to prove that forgiveness was naive.

Do you want to live your life like there is always something negative lurking, just waiting to pounce on you? Or do you want to live your life like there will be many lessons in all shapes and sizes, some more comfortable than others, and that is worth living it with a free heart?

Once again, we see forgiveness peeking at us, blink blink blink... little doe eyes charm us once again, and as we move closer, a memory appears. Forgiveness eyes us closely for our reaction and readies itself for the dart and dash. We place our hand over our heart and release it, putting a little blessing of love on all who were involved and let it go. Finally, forgiveness comes to us, curls up in our chest, and lets out a little sigh. Relief is ours at last.

Reflection

Whew! You made it!

You got down and dirty with your beastly feelings and came out the other side. Oh, you will still have to work on emotional awareness daily, but that's okay. It will take practice, and you won't always meet the challenge the way you want to. Forgive yourself. Try again.

The idea is that now you have become more aware, you are less reactive and more reflective. You can determine what is setting you off, then pause and give yourself some room to think about it. Get some space if you need to. The great thing is, by giving yourself the room to feel your feelings truly, you clear the playing field and become more objective.

You will find meaningful words to express yourself calmly and healthily. As a result, you have a better chance of being heard. You are setting an example for better etiquette around disagreements. You can lovingly say difficult things without causing damage. Creating a new habit that shows positive results gives you more confidence in yourself while dealing with confrontation.

How great is that?!

Knowing what you are feeling right now is the first step to moving up the scale to feeling better. There is no right or wrong way to feel. Just begin to process it, write about it, give your pillow a healthy fluffing if you must. Then, find your inner voice to guide you as you move through that emotion, and before you know it, you sense that you feel something else. Something that feels better— even if it is only slightly.

Something remarkable begins to happen! You remember what it feels like to feel better! The positive vibes are working! Holy shit, and hallelujah!

That feels awesome, doesn't it? Positivity, compassion, love, laughter, joy, appreciation, gratitude, relief.... they all grow from the release of negative emotions. They sprout up like little miracles at first because we thought they would never exist again. We didn't know those seeds were planted and just waiting for a bit of sunshine and water to begin growing. But there they are, and we get tickled at first sight of them.

You can feel good. You can do things that help that process along. You are ALLOWED, despite anything that may be going on with your loved one. Keep watering your garden and pluck out the weeds before they get too hardy. Give your attention to what feels like a healthy choice for you and follow your intuition. If it feels good, do it. If it feels negative, don't. Trust yourself to know the difference and keep steering your energy towards the positive.

If a weed gets away on you, and you fall into stinking thinking, examine your emotions and write it out. Determine where the feelings stem from, write out the reasons and your reactions, walk through the exercises I have given you again, then yank that prickly sucker out!

There will always be days where we struggle more than others, I can assure you. I still have them. More than I would like, but then I allow myself to learn and get back to the business of my self-care. Sing, dance, exercise, play with your dog, take a walk in the sunshine, watch a funny movie— whatever it takes to redirect your thinking.

It will get easier with time. The sprouts take a while to grow, and so do your new feeling good habits. But, as a solid foundation begins to form, you gain the self-confidence to handle life's challenges. You have a fresh perspective on addiction, your loved one's behavior, and your self-awareness now.

With awareness comes action. We must start making choices with these new tools to avoid falling back into our usual comfort zone. That hasn't been working, and we are sick of it anyhow.

In the next chapter...

We continue our positivity journey to understand the first of two new and healthy coping methods around addiction. You will finally understand what works, what doesn't, and why you keep moving forward.

Emotions Affirmation

My emotions are my inner guidance system
signaling what I want based on positive or
negative vibrations.
I trust my inner guidance system to direct me
for my highest good.
As I continue to heal, I know that my
confidence will grow, and I will feel what is
healthy for me.
I will take space to process my emotions when
they get intense and know that they are
temporary.
As I release negative emotion, I will look for a
better feeling point of relief until I feel calm
again.

Chapter Five

Detachment

It is easy to get stuck in a limiting pattern with addiction swirling around you. Round and round you go keeping the momentum going so debris doesn't fling off in all directions. But that is all it is— a limiting pattern of thinking.

We think we can't quit that job. We think we must stay in the house. We think we are too selfish. We think the world will collapse around us if we don't hide the addiction in our lives. BUT IT ISN'T TRUE. The sun comes up, we keep breathing, and we find solutions for breaking new ground. We have thought ourselves into a hole and believe there is no way out. But, if we could think ourselves onto one path, we can certainly think ourselves onto a different one. Maybe it's another hole; perhaps that one isn't quite so deep.

Solutions don't come all at once, and shazam— you have a new life.

No, it comes by making minor changes to your way of thinking. It's about gaining a little more confidence in yourself by making one positive change, just one. Then tomorrow, another.

You build your new life motto with hope, your newfound knowledge with eagerness for change. Then, finally, the Universe notices that something isn't quite so clogged, and blessings begin to flow. Kindness comes more effortless, and you realize that when you feel happier, the more people around you feel happier too.

You grow! You shine! You fuck up and laugh about it! Your sense of humor is that much funnier.

Then one day— LOOK AT THAT! You have created a path of healing and feel the blessing of relief.

Finding your new routine will encourage others to do the same. Cause and effect, baby! There is a movement towards love and empowerment, healing, and health. Without fixing or solving anything for the people around us, our loved ones may start making positive changes. By not living your life based on their success or failure, they see that you can love them despite their struggles. You have learned what you can participate in or not, based on how it makes you feel, and know that if it doesn't feel good, it doesn't belong inside the walls of your boundaries.

One day, you may realize that your path doesn't line up with theirs any longer, and that is okay too. Unfortunately, though, there may still be a grief process.

Without judgment, labels, or guilt, everyone gets to walk their path, and you realize you are happier for not carrying those things around with you. It is easier to let go and be happy without those negative emotions and the vibration it creates.

That is something I discovered after my divorce. I went through a great deal of judgment, guilt, and shame for many years before I realized the significance of that lesson.

If I have learned anything from the family session discussions around addiction, I finally realized my self-worth and power one day at a time. It allows my loved ones to evolve, with or without sobriety, which doesn't change who I am.

"These mountains that you are carrying, you were only supposed to climb."

Najwa Zebian

I would try to move mountains if I saw someone hurting or in trouble in my old way of thinking. I thought, "I'll just remove the obstacle, and things will be easier for them."

Much like pushing a car out of the snowdrift. With addiction, it doesn't work that way. It didn't occur to me that my loved ones needed to acknowledge the mountain and put their own damn hiking boots on. Eventually, I clued in, and if my loved ones were making healthy choices for themselves, I was willing to strap my boots on and climb the mountain with them. But only if I was going that way.

We deserve to be free of addiction and codependent coping mechanisms, and it starts with a truly genuine desire for change. I can't make you change. I couldn't make any of my four loved ones change. BUT I can change myself. I can help people believe in themselves enough to start the process. I wasn't willing to do their work, though, nor was I willing to pretend there wasn't a problem.

When we tried everything we could think of, and it didn't work, we hit the end of our rope feeling like we were the ones who failed. (There is no such thing as failure, by the way!) So we try a different angle, a more direct approach, the silent treatment, ignoring the problem, or addressing the issue in every other sentence. All that effort with no apparent positive results— it sucks!

I've personally tried it all, and I wore myself out doing it. I'm sure you have too. But like me, I bet you were doing it from a caretaking standpoint and weren't aware. And we have been doing it for so long that it seems like second nature. So much worse, it's a super whammy if your child is the one in addiction. So, what do we do?

You may have guessed it by now, but we must examine our typical reactions. Get out that lovely journal and begin answering the following questions:

- **When I suspect that my loved one has been using/drinking, I react by_____?**
- **When I suspect using/drinking, I feel _____.**
- **When I discover that my loved one has been using/drinking, I react by_____?**

- When   I   discover   using/drinking,   I   feel
_____.
- When I confront my loved one about my suspicions, what happens?
- When I confront my loved one about my discovery, what happens?
- What is my response to my loved one's reaction?
- How often does this cycle happen?
- What do I do to avoid fallout or conflict from this cycle?
- List what hasn't worked to break the cycle.
- List what has worked to break the cycle.

Do you have a better picture of where the storm of addiction sucked you inside? Do you have a little more knowledge of where the pitfalls are?

When I first started examining my reactions, I discovered that my anger flared within seconds of any sign of dishonesty, disrespect, or accusations that came my way. No way was I going to tolerate any bullshit from anyone. Yet, I found myself staying put as this repeatedly played out in front of me. It wasn't just with one relationship; it was a habit from others too. Their addiction wasn't about me, and I knew it, but it gave me room to make excuses.

I got mad, gave them shit, and got angrier until I was yelling and not listening to a single word. My loved one wasn't listening either, and we fed off each other. Before my loved one left for the recovery center, it was happening daily. We didn't get anywhere, and I was going crazy while the drinking was non-stop. I was always honest, but it turned into cutting remarks about their behavior. I played nice, and it didn't work, so I played hardball. It didn't change anything because I was still playing.

With a lot of reflection and a few new tricks up my sleeve, I discovered just how much I was caretaking everyone and everything in my life. I had to find a way to raise my kids without doing everything for them. I had to delegate more at work with reasonable expectations. But, I couldn't control poor behavior or their outcomes. I realized that if there is value in my tough lessons, there must be value in my loved ones' tough lessons too.

Who was I to decide that for anyone other than myself? I want people to discover self-esteem for themselves. I want them to see their value and gain confidence as they make their way. I want to see them thrive and be happy.

That meant, as uncomfortable as it may be, I had to see them fail too.

It's not an easy task, let me tell you. When the shit hits the fan, and you do nothing but allow the events to unfold, you are allowing your loved ones to experience the full effect of their actions. It's their learning opportunity to determine what their next step may be. They may need to learn this lesson repeatedly too. The temptation will be to appease the situation and ease your suffering, which is selfish in its own way.

Our goal is to redirect our focus and typical reaction away from addiction and towards positive behavior. It is watering the garden and trusting the sun and soil to do their job. We allow our loved ones to handle themselves, and we start getting our life back. The more we do this, the more objective we become and less attached to the outcome.

Detachment with Love

The term detachment gets thrown around a lot around the treatment of addiction. You hear it in counseling and read it in books, but sometimes we don't understand what they mean.

Detachment:
"the freedom from prejudice or partiality" and **"aloofness, as from worldly affairs or from the concerns of others"**

How does it relate to us?

Attachment is personally owning the experiences and emotions of others, often to the detriment of our health. Not only do we care, but we are also personally invested in the outcome even though we have no control over the people or situations we have latched on to. It can be present in any relationship and not reserved for those dealing with addictions.

Again, attachment styles stem from childhood and are another book for another day. I will say, though, attachments aren't the end-all-be-all of human behavior in relationships, just like codependent behavior or addiction are simple matters.

Detachment removes us from the ownership of emotions, physical reactions, problems, and substance abuse of our loved ones. We focus on our lane instead of dancing a marionette performance with addiction as the puppet master. We can only be in control of and responsible for ourselves. We still care, are still human, and want the very best for our loved ones. Detachment is saying, "I no longer allow your journey to take priority over mine. I can no longer intervene, chaperon, or hide for my loved one's sake."

In our hearts, we know that we feel responsible if we don't prevent the worst-case scenario from happening— whatever that may be. We need a roof over our heads, food on the table, and money to support ourselves. But, unfortunately, our strength becomes our loved one's crutch, and they lose sight of what it is like to walk on their own.

Detachment is no longer holding up those who lean on us in unhealthy ways, and that goes for any relationship we have in our lives. Our adult children could decide to live with us until they are thirty, but at some point, the fledgling must realize they have wings of their own. It is the same with those in addiction.

Fail or flourish, our loved ones live their own life without our interference. So, in a way, my loved one decided I was no longer their crutch with a very crude and immediate decision to go into detox. They didn't even see me to say goodbye. But, unfortunately, I was the one wobbling around without balance after this quick change of pace. I developed my own lean to counter their weight, and I fell flat on my face with them gone— and it took years to right myself again.

Our loved ones experience it when detachment is fast. It can make or break the outcome of their addiction, but with detachment, you lose the idea of control over their life or their death. You are on your journey as they are on theirs.

What is at stake if we don't find detachment?

Our own mental or physical health can become perilous. We may even die before the person in addiction does! Healing the entire family in and around addiction is essential because we leave our children to inherit the same behaviors and struggles with addiction and codependency without breaking the cycle. If we hit our breaking point, our kids will have two parents out of the picture.

When we learn detachment, we are as vulnerable as a fledgling too. But, at the same time, we must leave the comfort of our nest to make our way. Thus, detachment is the first step to saving ourselves.

Love is not something we just do in terms of actions. Instead, love is something we feel intensely, and it is impossible to describe accurately. It just is. We feel it as a powerful connection to each other. From that feeling, our actions follow, including detachment. Codependency uses love as an excuse for caretaking, controlling, and making conditional demands. Loving detachment is a healthy response or action to unhealthy addiction behavior.

Detachment with love is saying, "I will let go without judgment or blame. Even though I love you, I allow you to excel or learn the hard way without changing the outcome or making it easier for you. And I will make sure to take care of myself now."

Detachment feels, well— heartless. Tough love feels like the opposite of love, but it allows our loved ones the learning experiences that we have perhaps buffered them from before. If they don't learn to get sober and find their legs for themselves, they will never believe in themselves enough to flourish. Instead, they will insist that they need a crutch for the rest of their lives— because, let's face it, they were addicted to our help, too!

But if we don't find a way to let go, the cycle of addiction will play on with no end in sight. So we just continue going in crazy circles trying to fix everything.

"Detachment does not mean you should own nothing. It means that nothing should own you."

Deepak Chopra

As parents, we understand detachment when kids learn to walk, fall on their little bum, and cry. So we smile, cuddle them a little and encourage them to try again.

We don't think, "That's okay, baby, I'll do all the walking for you. I'll make sure you never feel any pain." We know that isn't possible.

We allow our children to learn, even if some bumps and bruises are involved. It's a process we understand in parenthood but can lose track of in codependent behavior. It sounds like this. "I will only feel good if you are okay, so I will make sure everything is okay for the both of us." Sound familiar?

Detachment is looking at our child with loving encouragement, empathy, and complete faith they will not only figure it out, but they will also master it!

It is no different for The Addicted. However, we react differently to our loved ones because we believe they are fully capable of thinking for themselves as adults and mistakenly get too emotionally involved in their healing process. By that I mean, we own it to the point of sacrificing ourselves over the outcome. The more we do the work for them, the less they do for themselves.

Detachment can be challenging, especially because many of our hopes and dreams intertwine in our relationship with our spouse or children. We dream of the holidays, graduations, weddings, and children, and when we have to detach ourselves from them, it threatens our dreams. We hold on tighter or longer just to keep our hope of happiness alive. Our grip squeezes out the possibilities for greater happiness because the people we love need to get healthy before it can happen. But we don't know how to trust unknowns, do we? The unknowns held some unpleasant surprises.

Sometimes detachment is slow and careful. We recognize that the situation is fragile. While it is a bit like taking the band-aid off slowly, the risk of a face plant is a very real tragedy waiting to happen. It was the case with one of my loved ones. I knew that if I made abrupt changes to move, sell the house and cause immediate upheaval, they wouldn't be safe. It was the hardest thing I have ever had to do for my self-care.

It was also the healthiest decision I had to make, and it makes me sad to even say it. There was a real risk of my mental health declining further until I was no longer myself. I was absorbing illness every day, and everything that I tried to do to stay healthy wasn't working. I finally had to follow my instincts, but I did it over many months.

It was a damn fragile time.

It's detachment with love. It was without judgment and carefully considered baby steps to let go with surety. It isn't about being cruel or harsh, though it feels that way to our loved ones when they are used to someone managing the stress in their lives. It's taking all our love and emanating it without doing anything for anybody else. That's right. We don't have to DO anything to love someone or be loved.

Loving someone is not about how much one person can do for another. Our loved one doesn't have to do anything for us, not even getting sober. What we do or don't do doesn't affect our feelings for the people in our lives either. So you know that detachment is simply letting go of the concrete idea about the outcome and loving our people through life, whether in good times or bad, within the healthy boundaries we set. We allow the Universe to guide our loved ones, and we love ourselves enough to do the same.

Some days, I didn't handle this so well, and I needed my space just to be okay. It left my kids without me for periods of time that made me feel selfish and absent. But, realizing that I am not perfect in my actions, I can relate to how my loved ones may feel about how their choices affected their children.

Detachment has allowed me to maintain a relationship with my loved ones on certain levels, and we continue to operate within boundaries. When I catch myself slipping, I readjust my actions without beating myself up.

Detachment with Our Children

believe it's more challenging when one of our children is struggling with addiction. We are battling a formidable instinct to protect them. We've caught them before they hit the pavement when they were little, saved them as they fell down the stairs, and nursed their wounds when we weren't there to catch them. How many of you felt guilty for being absent when our kids broke their bones, got bullied, or had their Halloween candy stolen?

I sure did. I had an overpowering urge to protect my children, and it felt like an actual failure when I couldn't. My extra crazy mothering instincts may stem from experiencing a dramatic accident when I was sixteen. I had just driven around the corner in a quiet neighborhood to realize that someone had run over a dog that ran out in front of a large work truck. Then I realized that it was a child, not a dog in a pink sweater, and I never got that image out of my head.

When I became a mom, my protective instincts were on fire. I was holding on tight, and I would keep them safe at all costs. That isn't a unique goal by any stretch, but I was fierce about it. As my kids got older, and especially as teens, this instinct was difficult for me because they were choosing things that could bring harm to themselves. I just couldn't handle that idea. I owned the outcome of their lessons like they were mine, and I had no tolerance for risky behavior.

Teenagers and young adults have peer pressure, societal demands, and developing frontal lobes. Our kids don't make rational decisions until their twenties, and if addiction is already present, denial can be so much worse. They can be impulsive, experimental, defiant, and sneaky, leading to trouble even without addiction. Teenagers and young adults rebel against their parents, eager to leave the nest, but need mommy and daddy when the world gets intimidating. With addiction, it's multiplied and amplified. It becomes deafening in our lives.

As parents, we lose track of the difference between healthy parenting, being supportive, or codependent behavior. Completely understandable! Compounding an already complex issue, add any kind of mental or behavioral disorders to the equation, and you've got hell on wheels— like me.

Detachment may be possible one day and not so much the next. It takes practice. Forgive yourself and try again. Keep trying. Be honest with yourself about what you are allowing and what to address head-on. Enlist your spouse, friends, and family to participate too. It is best to give kiddos consistency, or they can take advantage of well-meaning people in their lives. Don't forget to include them in the conversation of your boundaries, consequences, and loving detachment.

It doesn't matter who we love or our relationship; we need to see our actions in the cycle and start letting them go. We must lose the controlling tendencies and realize that we are only making ourselves miserable for it.

Now we understand how we typically react when addiction throws us off the deep end, and we know how it makes us feel. We also know that there must be a better way and why detachment is so necessary. So the next question becomes: HOW?

Detachment Steps

Detachment is necessary, as we just realized, but we need it because of two separate issues. One— our caretaking has overloaded us with responsibilities, and we have acted in ways that weren't in our best interests. Two — we are so emotionally invested in everything our loved one is doing that we forget our wellbeing, dreams, desires, and goals. Both are heartbreaking and exhausting.

The following exercises will deal with each of these issues in a way that shows you just how much control you have been trying to maintain and what it will be like to release it.

We will go over the importance of boundaries, but for now, we will go through some detachment steps to use in conjunction with the boundaries we set in the next chapter.

Settle into your healing space and grab your journal, a highlighter, a red pen, and your regular pen. Do the following:

Make a list of <u>everything</u> you do in a single day, week, and then a month. Include tasks, self-care, and responsibilities. Include things like paying bills, groceries, shoveling the walk— anything that has fallen solely on you now that addiction is in the picture.

Go through this list and highlight anything that your loved one used to handle. For example, if it was a shared task, but you do it alone now, highlight it too.

With your regular pen, circle all the self-care items on your list.

How does this exercise make you feel? Write them out.

Does this list look like there is a balance between your own responsibilities/needs and your loved ones'? For example, is there a lot of highlighter on the page? How often did you take a walk, go to yoga, read a book, get your nails done, see your friends, or volunteer for your favorite charity?

It seems like a simple task because we keep them all itemized in our heads, but when we see them on paper, it's shocking to see who, what, when, and where we prioritized our energy. How many items were not your responsibility at all? It is a bit of a wake-up call when you realize how lopsided your life has become. It doesn't include the disagreements, the nights alone, the missed concerts, or the lack of sex. It doesn't account for missing date night or family time with the kids. Instead, the substance or habit of choice is always present and robbing us of a quality life.

Next, take a red pen and circle anything that you can delegate. Don't be afraid to hand out responsibility. People are more capable than you allowed them to be. Notice how much of the list you changed. Can you delegate some more? Notice whether the list feels more balanced. Do you need to revise anything?

Journal about what happens if you delegate tasks, but they don't get completed? What will you do? Journal about what happens after everyone completes their tasks? What will you do? How do you feel now?

It may seem like a mild exercise for some, but this may be difficult for those of us who became obsessed with doing everything ourselves. Being the powerhouse of magnificent accomplishments is a fantastic ability, but it isn't easier, faster, or more accurate to do it all yourself. I've tried.

If you have children of a proper age who don't do their chores, make them earn a phone or game time or an allowance. They may resist a bit when you put your foot down. It can also be emotionally challenging for you to handle until they learn the new routine. That's okay. Explain why you need their participation and how it makes you feel when they don't cover their responsibilities. Don't forget to tell them how you feel when they do carry out their tasks too.

If you feel that you can have a decent conversation with your loved one about sharing the responsibilities around the house, then make sure you choose your moment. It may work or just irritate the crap out of them because they don't realize how little they are doing. But, if it makes it easier, place one hand on your heart while you talk. It is offering your words from your heart and helps open a channel between you. Besides, the more likely you are to start a fight, the less likely you are to rebalance your responsibilities.

Your loved one isn't likely to take on a giant list that you thrust at them, nor is that quite the design of the exercise. It was to make you more aware of all you are doing, not throw it in your loved one's face about slacking off. Work towards change in small steps, without getting in anyone's face or acting overly emotional. Small changes got you both into this situation, and both of you have to start slow to get out of it.

Success comes in small milestones that are more manageable for everyone, and it leads to bigger wins. And if they aren't on board? Then, it could be time to consider whether your relationship is meeting your needs equally. Consider seeing a counselor for additional support and clarity. There is more information on professional help in Chapter Eight.

Regardless of what you could remove from your plate, you are aware of everything you are trying to pull off in your life. The proof is on the page. Does it overwhelm you just looking at it? I know I couldn't believe my eyes when I examined my list. Who was I trying to be?? Wonder Woman?

When I read my list, I was pissed. I thought it was all my loved one's fault for putting me in that position, for adding to my load every day, and not giving a shit how upset I was about it. Blame, blame, and more blame. I wasn't going to admit that I had put myself in this position and firmly planted myself to stay. Instead, I was going to prove to them all the ways that I was right and that they needed to change. Sounds healthy, right? Yeah, well, what I was really doing was handing over my power to my loved one's addiction and then getting upset for feeling powerless.

When I let all my resentment fade away, I realized that I could make changes for myself, with or without anyone's permission. I had a choice. It was time to start making them.

1. Make a list of all the things you can change about your daily routine while eliminating caretaking. Then your weekly routine. Your monthly routine.

2. Write out what the consequences of change could be, positive and negative.

3. Write out your worst-case scenario. Then, include what you would do if that were to happen. How does this make you feel?

4. Write out your best-case scenario. Then, include what you would do if that were to happen. How do you feel now?

As you move through your list, you will notice which will pose a significant problem in your life. It may bring up intense feelings of fear, anxiety, despair, or resistance. Write down these feelings as well. It is okay to sit in the moment and allow them to pass, examining the origin of your feelings. Take your time! Go slow rather than give in to the impulse to race through. It is your chance to process with clarity, gently realizing that you may not have all the solutions right now, but you are strong enough to handle anything that comes up.

Now we need to understand why we have been doing all this wild running around. Why have we nurtured people who can take care of themselves?

Caretaking Plan

It's nice to feel needed, isn't it? There is some kind of karmic reward for helping someone, isn't there? It is morally pleasant to be giving and feel the warmth of appreciation returned. The more we offer, the more gratitude comes our way and the better we feel. The better we feel, the more we want that. The more we want that, the more we seek out ways to be giving. The more ways we seek out happiness and gratitude, the more fun we have. The more fun we have must mean we are on the right track.

With a healthy balance, this is perfectly loving and appreciative. However, an unhealthy dynamic can lead to seeking self-worth by relying solely on the loving reactions we receive from others. If you only feel good about yourself by making others happy, you inadvertently land on a slippery slope. Especially when your tank is empty, and you don't have anything left to give— or are flat broke.

And then, our loved ones get so used to this giving nature that they forget to show their gratitude. So it gives us a little jolt, but we override it by saying to ourselves, Oh, that's okay, they must be busy or tired. I don't need anything in return."

We continue giving until it becomes caretaking, trying harder when we don't get the reaction we want, and appreciation becomes a thing of the past. Yet, we still seek it out. Until one day, they rely entirely on our giving nature and ability to solve their problems, and we are miserable in full-blown codependent behavior. It's manipulating the circumstances for a positive response because asking for what we need and want is risky. If they say no, we feel rejected and still don't have our needs met to boot. Addiction doesn't often leave room for constructive conversations, does it?

We get frustrated; maybe we say something, maybe we don't. Resentment builds, but we keep going to ridiculous extremes to help. Avoiding catastrophe saves you and your loved ones from dire consequences, but really, you want attention and the same amount of effort from them.

Pretty soon, you are fucking mad but have no idea how all of this got so out of whack. You gained weight, your hair started falling out, and you complained to anyone who would listen. Even when you aren't physically managing all the responsibilities or trouble-shooting issues, your mind is constantly racing and focused on them.

It was me in a nutshell. I even joked how nice one of those white cuddle jackets with the straps would be while I sat in a padded room and got hand-fed Jell-o. Jenny, the Giver, was now Jenny the Scraggly Hermit. I had nothing left for anyone, and I didn't welcome any additional requests of my time or energy.

I kept giving away my love and energy when my bucket was empty. Finally, nothing was left for me, and I hit bottom with a serious pout on my face.

Answer these questions in your journal:

- **What are your feelings and typical reaction when you see someone who needs help?**

- Is it healthy? Why?
- Is it unhealthy? Why?
- Do you seek positive reinforcement by giving in place of healthy conversations?
- What would it look like to have a constructive conversation about your needs and wants?
- Name a time when your loved one had a difficult situation, but you stepped in to help. Why did you choose to help?
- How did this make it easier for them?
- How was this a healthy/unhealthy choice for you?
- What would have happened if you didn't help them?
- How often does this happen in a day? A week? A month?
- What happens if you no longer do this?

"ALL HELL WILL BREAK LOOSE, THAT'S WHAT!" I'm sure that was your first reaction. So I am with you there.

It got to the point that I was only okay if everyone else was taken care of. That included The Addicted in my life, my kids, and everyone at work. Any confrontation or problem overwhelmed me, and I did everything I could to avoid that feeling. I pleased as many people as possible to the point of feeling hysteric whenever there was an issue. But that was on the inside. I projected my friendly and smiling personality outward, trying so hard just to hold it together long enough to manage my way through until I got home—Jenny to the rescue. Jenny will fix it.

I was damn good at it too. But when the night finally got quiet, and I was alone, I cried myself to sleep and passed out hard.

I truly felt that if I didn't take care of everything, I would be responsible for the outcome. I worked my ass off to ensure everything appeared to be running normally at work, but I was run ragged and barely hanging on if you looked under the surface.

I had to examine what I was doing that contributed to my situation. Then the question came up, "Why am I doing this to myself?" I was overachieving at the caretaking game when I should have focused on my happiness. I also had to release any feelings of selfishness because that was only going to keep me trapped.

It's your turn.

- **Write out all the ways you try to make it better when problems arise.**
- **Write out all the ways you try to fix people.**
- **Write out all the ways you try to save people.**
- **How do you feel while you are doing this?**
- **Why do you feel the caretaking urge?**
- **How would you feel to allow the person to figure out a solution for themselves? Why?**
- **Instead, what do you plan to do when you feel tempted to 'fix' or 'make it better?'**

Survival instincts are there for a reason. In the eye of the storm, they never switch off. Our fight, flight, freeze, and fawn response is intense when we constantly feel threatened, so why and how we got into this frantic habit is understandable. But our perception is also limiting our vision and finding imminent threats everywhere we look.

You will notice the 'fixing' feeling the next time a moment arises. This time, you may pause and consider your options. Maybe you will remember a better alternative in your best interest and choose to walk away. You will know what feels good to you.

Here are some examples:

1. "I will not clean up other people's messes."

2. "I will take a walk or read a book when I realize they have been drinking."

3. "I will consider how I feel before I react."

4. "I will meditate when I feel the negative impact of my loved one's addiction."

5. "I will make myself a cup of tea and have a constructive conversation when I'm calm."

These are not big life changers, nor are they very profound. They are simple decisions not to interact when emotions run high, or a survival instinct is triggered. Instead, it adds self-care to a routine by taking a step back to pause, reflect, consider and then act.

The idea of detachment is not to stuff down your feelings or excuse behaviors that you know are unsafe or unhealthy. It is also not a form of manipulation where you refuse to do X, Y, Z until they do A, B, C. It is a loving gesture you give to yourself despite the other person's actions. It's making a choice regardless of theirs without ultimatums and being okay if your choices don't align. Your process will not be in a straight line as it can take a while to build up self-esteem. You are practicing the act of grace, inviting it into your daily expression of self.

As you get more practiced with negative interactions, your loved one may start to realize something is different.

It may elicit a couple of responses.

They may begin to watch their words, their actions becoming a little more civilized, and they show signs of awareness around their addiction. So your seemingly aloof behavior jars the crutch, and they can't lean so heavily on you anymore.

Or... they decide you have betrayed them. Unfortunately, some people will not accept anything less than a mother/caretaker figure in their lives, which may mean a rocky existence for you. While it is not acceptable for anyone to act in an abusive manner, this too may be a sign that they are becoming more aware— in a rapidly uncomfortable environment they can't stand. Their addictive behavior doesn't work anymore, and they recover, or they have to find a different environment to operate within their coping mechanism.

You may even see the worst of their addiction before they begin to realize that your changes are more about loving space rather than punishment. I assure you that detaching with action is the only way to break the cycle. The Addicted will surely not react well because this feels like abandonment, which is scary and touches on the painful layers behind their harmful habits. It isn't easy on The Affected either, because our caretaking came from a loving place, so to stop feels like we are abandoning them and causing them pain. I certainly felt intense guilt for this.

I also know that detachment is the answer to happiness when addiction or neediness is present. It is the personal freedom and grace we give ourselves, where we previously thought we had to hold on tight. There is more power in letting go than the stranglehold of fear.

Without the gift of loving detachment, I believe my loved ones would continue ignoring the consequences of their actions. One would likely have overdosed or gotten killed by hanging out in dangerous crowds. Instead, they got sober and now appreciate all life has to offer.

Reflection

We have been married to the idea of 'what is' in our loved one's addiction, playing our part and suffering the same consequences as them. We may have survived, but we aren't happy. So we began looking for answers, thinking that we needed to solve the addiction to remedy our situation. Now we know that we have our own addictive habits to resolve to gain improvement in our lives.

I know that is precisely what I thought when I demanded to go to the addiction counselor. But what I discovered, after a long twisty road and a healthy dose of shock, was none of this was my job.

All the bandages in the world were not going to patch up a person who kept cutting themselves open. I realized that if my loved ones' problems weren't my fault, failing to fix them wasn't either. I certainly had my own issues to worry about, and no one was coming to my rescue. Nor would I have appreciated anyone trying to take over my decision-making either. My nagging, pleading, begging, and yelling were just a control tactic with people who needed to handle their own stuff.

I had spent a great deal of time trying to prevent catastrophe, so of course, I would think I wasn't getting it right when things continued to get worse. But the more I saw the truth, the more conscious I was of where I needed to be objective.

Detaching with love didn't mean that I ignored the addiction or my loved one's health. It meant that I was more unbiased about the circumstances or the outcome. I let judgment go and just observed it with a bit of distance. I didn't take it all so personally when I stopped owning their pain. I began to feel better, bit by bit, one day at a time. I finally saw the first glimmer of hope when I thought I would never feel hopeful again.

Understanding detachment for yourself will be a process of trial and error. It was essential to become aware of your typical reactions so that you could choose a new course of action. You will likely find yourself saying no far more often— and repeatedly for a while. Deciding not to participate doesn't mean your loved one won't pull out all stops to convince you that you are the problem. They could accuse you of causing the upset and attempt to make you return to the way it was— which was more comfortable for them.

In the next chapter...

You will see that strict boundaries are essential to creating the space you need to be healthy. Without boundaries, you will be pushed back into depreciating tactics until you are back to square one.

Detachment Affirmation

I am a peaceful observer of my surroundings.
From this viewpoint, I am witness to my
beautiful journey with love in my heart.
I allow my choices to reflect my goals for
personal healing, growth, and joy.
I allow the actions of my loved ones to be of
their choosing, and I can love them regardless.
I am safe to let them stumble or fall as I want
nothing more than for them to discover their
self-worth.
I am free to decide what is best for me.

Chapter Six

Boundaries

Let's have a show of hands. How many of us have heard the term 'setting healthy boundaries?' I think it's fair to say most of us have, whether we were parenting, training our puppy, or dealing with addiction. Sounds good, doesn't it? Just set that healthy boundary with rules and stipulations, and all will fall into place.

Yes, I am sarcastic because, honestly, this was the easiest thing to say but the hardest thing to pull off.

The skill of setting boundaries came up in our family sessions. First, it was a revelation that I was setting healthy boundaries with a loved one when I got legal custody of their child or refused access when they were using. I honestly thought I was just a maniacal bitch over their drinking problem and felt tremendous guilt for being that mean, even with a child's safety at stake. But, it turns out that was the healthy thing to be doing. Who knew?!

I got shaky in setting boundaries when parenting my kids and with loved ones in addiction. I would get overwhelmed entirely when my kids kicked up a stink, repeatedly demanding to get what they wanted, and either I would lose my temper completely, or I would give in. There was no calm determination while they figured out mom wasn't going to budge.

It was black and white when a child's welfare was at stake, but a very grey area when it was my intimate relationships. I saw past my loved ones' pain and subsequent coping behaviors. They experienced abuse, neglect, mental health disorders, and abandonment, and I didn't judge them for having a hard time. BUT, I ignored plenty of red flags while putting their needs before my own. As a result, my boundaries were soft, and I took the brunt of the consequences.

Every time I turned around, I was losing out.

It didn't mean my loved ones were terrible people, uncaring or abusive. On the contrary, they are beautiful souls, but people in pain hurt the ones they love the most, intentional or not.

After the family sessions at the recovery center, I called my loved one out on it a lot more, refusing to drive them around or stay in a messy apartment. I didn't give in as much to demands when my loved ones could handle their needs themselves. So there was more tension between us too.

In the past, I avoided tension or conflict with all my might. In hindsight, my anxiety stemmed from the push-pull of my loved one's demands while I was trying to set boundaries. A lack of solid boundaries made it too easy for my loved one to ignore the need for help, for family members to make me the scapegoat around their addiction, and for poor behavior with a mental health condition.

So, lovely reader, I believe that while none of us want to go through more pain and discomfort for the sake of a new set of rules, we also know, deep down, that we are bound for endless suffering if we don't.

What is a Boundary?

What are boundaries, and how do we put them in place?

A boundary is a safety zone that protects our needs, wants, feelings, and values. They help maintain physical, mental, and emotional health. Boundaries are also essential for building and nurturing healthy relationships between me, you, and us as they differentiate between the three.

Whether we realize it or not, we already have boundaries in our lives. It's not wearing specific colors, how much is too much food, or when to say no thank you to solicitors. They are easy when it isn't upsetting or involving a loved one's demands.

A boundary is a line in the sand. It is the 'you can go no further' point, where the answer is firmly NO. And the only way they work is to state the rules, consequences, and reasons clearly for all to follow. But, of course, that means you must follow them too; otherwise, it isn't a boundary—it's your blurry attempt at being tough on the people in your life.

Why are they so bloody important anyhow?

Without boundaries, we become the roadkill in every need, wish, desire, demand, please, and thank you from everyone in your life. If you give in to everything they ask from you, then there is no room for you in the equation. As a result, we become unhealthy in our obsession to make everything okay, never looking out for ourselves. As a result, we lose our identity entirely as someone with unique tastes and preferences.

Simply stated, with love— without boundaries, no one will learn a damn thing, including you.

First, let's try a little exercise with your journal to define what you need to feel safe, happy, and healthy.

Draw a house in the middle of your page, like you used to draw in grade one. Add a roof and door, but leave out the windows. We will be writing inside this simple drawing. Write single-word phrases inside the house that describe what you need to feel safe, happy, and healthy in your life. (For example, you could write sobriety, exercise, books, meditation, tea, nature, love. You can make it artistic, linear, random...anything you like.)

Around the outside of the house, write single-word phrases for all the things that are not welcome. (For example, you could say drinking, drugs, abuse, blame, anger, judgment.)

Write in terms of actions and behaviors, not people. Don't exclude people with this task but instead simply identify what actions fit in your inner sanctum. I like this metaphor because we get to decide what we open the door to or not.

Take a good look at your values and consider where you have sacrificed to keep the peace. It is now your guideline to know what you will allow in your house or what you won't. You can use this tool to practice saying NO when tempted to let negative actions or emotions impede your values.

Having this visualization helps to keep you more focused on your priorities as well. When something doesn't fit inside your house, that's your signal to redirect or detach from the situation.

Again, it takes some practice to see where you tend to cave in or cater to your loved one's demands. Conversely, it takes practice to know where you break your boundary too. First, you must recognize the patterns that have repeated themselves and your reaction. Second, you must recognize the repeating patterns and your loved one's response. Once you see it with more clarity, you can start changing your reactions to align with your values. Your loved ones will likely buck this to some degree because they are used to the routine, but the more you stick to your new tune, they will eventually sing a new song with you. Or quit bothering you.

Answer the following questions in your journal:

• **What are the rules that I have in my house and with my loved ones?**

• **What are the consequences if they don't comply?**

• **When I feel someone has crossed a line or broken a rule, I react by _____.**

• **When my loved one is confronted with breaking a rule, they react by _____.**

- **When this happens, do I typically stand my ground? Or do I cave in? Why?**
- **When I stand my ground, what happens?**
- **How do I feel when I stand my ground?**
- **When I cave in, what happens?**
- **How do I feel when I cave in?**

If you struggled a bit with this, I understand. You and me both. Every situation is unique, and we handle each of our relationships differently as well.

My children knew how to manipulate better outcomes when they wanted something or were trying to get out of punishment. One was particularly relentless and wouldn't accept any version of an outcome that wasn't of their own choosing. That comes with the territory of their mental health condition, though, and over the years, I got good at caving in to their demands to make it stop.

Of course, this wasn't the same in my romantic relationships, but I found myself compromising way more often than standing my ground. When it came to the important stuff on my list, like how I needed to be nurtured or treated, I quite often just took what I got and made do. I already held a mistaken belief I wasn't good enough, and when my needs weren't met, it added to that feeling. I wasn't happy. My attempts to discuss what I wanted and needed were often scoffed at or ignored. When I said no, or put my foot down, I felt guilty or selfish. If I got my way, it wasn't a pleasant compromise on my partner's part. Couples counseling would have been beneficial, but that was another unmet need that drastically affected my relationships.

It's an absolute flux, and it isn't fun to feel unimportant to the people we love the most. But life isn't supposed to be rigid either. We must find flexible solutions in healthy relationships to find balance. But the relationship(s) must get healthy first, which will take some work from both parties. We can't be healthy without the guidelines and boundaries we set for ourselves and insist that they be respected. A relationship will not thrive when one person sacrifices their needs or happiness to maintain the other.

When we clearly understand everyone's needs and values in a relationship, creating boundaries protects them. These needs and values aren't flimsy little things to disregard; they are our chosen fundamental rights. Therefore, anyone we allow in our lives must respect them, or they don't get to participate in it.

Setting Boundaries

A boundary is a line around a fundamental need for happiness, self-care, love, and respect. It is unique to every person, and it can be hard to navigate when boundaries are wishy-washy.

You wrote down what you valued and didn't, so it's time to understand what is at stake. Now you need to determine what your boundaries are. You will not take anything but complete respect when you say no, nor will you entertain anyone who is attempting to manipulate a different answer out of you. These are your rights, written by you and no one else gets to determine them for you, so, therefore, no one gets to adjust the boundary around them either.

Boundaries can be as simple as "I will not take care of anyone else until I have meditated and I refill my bucket." On the other hand, boundaries can be as profound as "I will not allow my safety to be at risk."

In your journal, write out a list of all personal boundaries that resonate with you. Base these on what you value but also on what you no longer want to experience. Take your time and write as many as possible. Remember, they not only protect you but nourish you also.

I have included examples of some of my boundaries to get you started. You can start small, working towards bigger ones as you get more practiced at maintaining them. You can also adjust these boundaries as you gain strength or discover new needs as you go. The only rule about setting boundaries is that you are honest with yourself, maintain them, and are clear with your loved ones on what they are.

Examples:

1. No alcohol or drugs are allowed on my property or in my house.

2. No one is allowed in my home under the influence of drugs or alcohol.

3. No one can borrow any money or belongings without permission.

4. No unannounced guests are permitted inside my house, and I will ask guests to leave should I feel uncomfortable at any time.

5. No one is permitted to be abusive towards me, my children, or my guests at any time.

6. I will not give money to buy alcohol or drugs.

7. No one will drive people under the influence of drugs and alcohol to purchase more.

8. No one will borrow money from me when they have spent all their money on drugs or alcohol.

9. I will not permit anyone to be dishonest with me about any of the above boundaries.

10. I will not remain in a relationship where my loved one is not in treatment or recovery for addiction.

11. If my loved one slips in their recovery, I will listen and support but let them create a plan to return to sobriety while reiterating my boundaries.

12. When a boundary is broken, I will maintain respect and ask the person(s) to leave or remove myself from the situation.

13. I will not alter my boundaries because of my loved one's upset or fear of the consequences of their actions.

14. I will not compromise my wellbeing or that of my children to maintain unhealthy relationships.

Coming up with your boundaries could take some time to design, but you customize them for you. As you write, you may realize where you are struggling more and where you may need to tighten it up.

Your loved ones must be clear on your boundaries because they can't read your mind. They are used to whatever worked with you before and may not even know how you are feeling. Therefore, presenting your new boundary is going to cause a ripple in the pond.

Keep your boundary list for yourself so that you can come back to it when things get wobbly. Each time an issue comes up where you typically compromised your wellbeing or happiness, clearly state:

I understand that you think what you are doing is acceptable. For me, it is not. I will no longer allow you to abuse my trust, my love, or my happiness for the sake of your addiction/poor behavior. If you continue to act in this manner, I will no longer participate in the conversation/relationship until you stop/get sober/treat me with respect. I have a boundary about _____ and I expect you to _____ or I will _____.

You can edit the statement to fit the situation and include how you will proceed. Remember to clearly state the boundary you are setting and your expectations without using them as a punishment or weapon. Show them the way with confidence and tell them why this is important to you.

Boundaries Aren't Easy

It all sounds good on paper— or even in counseling sessions. Know your rules, set your boundary, state your boundary, the boundary gets followed, wipe your hands and say, "There! I'm done!"

If we know anything, addiction makes master manipulators out of our loved ones, and we experience the worst of it. Of course, there are bosses, friends, business associates, and the guy at the liquor store who've heard their flavorful stories, but we are the ones in their lives. We experience the lying, storytelling, and straight-up bullshit way more often and up close.

Our loved ones borrow money that they say is for rent, but it gets spent on drugs or gambling. They tell us they are going to work, but they got fired three months ago and hung out feeling sorry for themselves in the lounge. They tell us we act crazy for constantly questioning their behavior then turn our words around until we believe we must be wrong.

Suddenly coming up with a list of rules they must abide by is a giant leap, especially for you. To set a boundary and mean it when you follow through on the consequence? Yeah, you will be the bad guy because there wasn't a problem until YOU did this to them. Our relationship is fine! You are overreacting, you can't prove anything, and I can do whatever I want! You won't go anywhere anyhow!

As I said before, I set some strict boundaries around one loved one in particular. Unfortunately, they tried to go around them in several ways and took advantage of any concessions. That soft boundary led them to kidnap their child after a visit, and it ended with neglect and abandonment before I got legal custody of their child.

When we don't uphold our boundaries, some dangerous things can happen.

No one wants to feel bad about themselves, nor do they want any kind of mayhem on their hands. That overwhelming bag of crapola will be a thing of the past once you begin affirming the new rules you have set for yourself.

Let's plot out some scenarios that will help strategize around your boundaries. This exercise will create a plan and anticipate where things might get a little tricky while you implement it.

Answer the following questions in your journal:

- **What are some ways that I can stand my ground without compromising my peace or happiness?**

- How would my loved one react?

- What are some ways to compromise without breaking my boundary or giving up my needs and values?

- How would my loved one react?

- What is the worst-case scenario if I stand my ground? Or compromise?

- What is the best-case scenario if I stand my ground? Or compromise?

As you write out your contingency plan, consider where you can compromise and where you cannot. Now is the time to consider how you will feel should you be faced with someone pushing your limits and how you will find ways to get support yourself. This is when self-care is needed the most. Detachment is challenged but is where all your practice will aid you.

Remember that you are the only one governing your rule book, so you also get to decide where you feel safe to compromise and where you don't.

For example:

A family kicks their daughter out over her drug addiction and the theft of money. Their boundary was that they would not allow her in the house while she was still using and in addiction. Sure enough, one frigid winter's night, they get a knock on the door to find their daughter evicted from her boyfriend's place, the shelter was packed, and she had nowhere to go. Faced with a life or death situation, she was not safe to turn away, but they could not allow her in the house because of their boundary. The compromise was to set their daughter up with blankets, a makeshift bed, and a heater in their sunroom with the stipulation she had to be gone by morning.

It sounds brutal— it honestly is. It is the worst feeling in the world to turn a loved one away because you can't participate in their choices. But the truth is, if you give in on this boundary, you are perpetuating the same issue to repeat itself. Your loved ones will continue their path in addiction until they hit rock bottom and begin to find resolutions for themselves. Our loved ones gain more knowledge through their conviction to help themselves than they will with our help.

Standing Firm

You've worked through some pretty tough stuff. Maybe you have already gotten started on upholding your boundaries in your relationships. Good for you! It takes a lot of bravery to make these changes in your life. It can be exhausting and lonely when no one understands why you've suddenly become a maniacal bitch/bastard. And it can be easy to fall back into old patterns because there was more comfort in what you knew than in unknown territory.

Instead of beating yourself up for the turmoil of your loved one's experience, you must remember detachment and allow them to learn this lesson too. The Addicted need to learn how to walk on their own with bumps and bruises, remember? They may fall on their face, but you can't buffer this for them without compromising your wellbeing to do it.

Jenny Truth: It isn't appropriate to set your boundary and then hug it out when your loved one gets upset. You aren't here to soothe their negative emotions, even if they say their feelings are hurt. Tears, anger, resentment, snotty comments, and dishes thrown aren't your problem. Those aren't your feelings, and you didn't cause them. They react from their perspective, and their view is, "If you loved me, you would give me what I want." You have done this, likely for too long, and it didn't work. Allow them to feel the impact of your NO.

Knowing that you are just starting to take steady steps yourself, it is essential to redirect any negative emotions that come up for you. When you recognize the niggling feeling that you are about to slip into that codependency jacket again, it is a good idea to enlist some positive affirmations.

Here are some examples to use when you are in the most challenging situations with your loved ones:

1. I acknowledge the hurt/confusion/pain I am feeling and know that their addiction is not my problem to solve. So I will take a walk in nature then have a cup of tea.

2. I acknowledge that they are really struggling right now. I will ground myself and meditate to reconnect.

3. I acknowledge that I am furious, and I will do a vigorous workout at the gym to burn off some steam.

4. Instead of swallowing my feelings, I will turn my attention to writing and allow them to flow onto the pages.

5. I will call my trusted friend for a good chat.

6. I will remain calm while allowing my loved ones to make decisions for themselves, no matter what they are.

7. I acknowledge that I can not control the outcome of their situation and will make an appointment with my counselor/support system to help stay focused on ME.

8. I will book a trip with my friend without worry or guilt.

9. I will garden/craft/build/create/clean/organize to help stay focused on my wellbeing.

10. With certainty, I will gain the confidence to know where I need to compromise and where I cannot.

11. I acknowledge that I am worthy, enough, loved, and safe no matter what my loved one is doing in their life.

Now write a set of action affirmations in your journal that best suit you and that you can put into practice whenever you are struggling with detachment or boundaries.

Who have we become around our loved one's addiction? Are we a wretched mess compared to the loving soul we know ourselves to be? Society duped us into thinking that you sacrifice all to 'make it work' when you love someone. We have then made every excuse in the book to ride out a life or death situation.

We don't always recognize the problem for what it is initially, and we sure don't know what the right thing to do is either. I certainly didn't, even when I appeared to have a plan. So I simply did the best I could under some extreme circumstances, and I'm gratefully on the other side of it with a better understanding of myself.

It comes down to knowing my own needs without feeling selfish. I am more aware of my superpowers now for having experienced the havoc of addiction. I can only be grateful at this stage, knowing that I have the chops to sort itself out for myself if heartache comes knocking. I learned boundaries in a ragged bushfire kind of way. I got burned, may have lost some hair, and likely didn't look too attractive, but I came out a warrior.

One last thought before we move on. As we expect others to honor and respect our boundaries, we must also do the same. Unfortunately, codependent behavior tends to override others' boundaries with the idea of "I know better than you do." Because the situation is serious, we think we have the right to march past someone's no to satisfy our need for security. Take a step back and consider where you need to respect your loved one's boundaries, and if they are willing, learn to navigate boundaries together.

Reflection

We had to understand detachment, so we didn't fly off the handle when getting our message across as we put our boundaries in place. We had to learn boundaries to understand the contrast between what we want in our lives and what we don't. By understanding what we don't want, we recognize when we were in danger of letting in those painful experiences. As a result, we finally gained the confidence to say what was happening and know, without a doubt, that the hardship of standing up for ourselves was worth it.

A new healthy outlook sets an excellent example for your children, friends, family, and loved ones. The more we stand our ground with honesty and respect, the less often we react from fear and anxiety. Instead, it begins to feel positive. Our loved one notices that things don't seem quite so intense, and they are catching on. It may take a while yet, but one day at a time.

The more you uphold your boundaries without lashing out, the easier it is to hear what your loved one has to say too. Perhaps they are now ready to start setting some healthy boundaries for themselves. It may be the beginning of awareness for them, and when that happens, you will respect their values as well.

Setting boundaries is the first and most crucial step into self-care. It takes your focus away from everything you believe is in the best interests of your loved one and starts you thinking about yourself again. But, unfortunately, you can only do you, and you learned that the hard way.

Now that you have had a taste of healthy selfishness, it is indeed time to start taking care of yourself. You've sacrificed enough. There has been a massive amount of damn good fun, relaxation, exciting books, and awesome friends waiting for you. There is a life out there, and it's all yours.

In the next chapter...

Chapter 7 is your hall pass from addiction into the classroom of self-care. You will delve into the world of your inner you, you know— the one that has been so desperately desperate to be set free again.

Boundaries Affirmation

My wellbeing is important to me.
I am creating a healthy space where I
experience laughter, love, joy, and peace.
I have no limitations in my healthy space, only
restrictions on what I allow to affect it.
I respectfully enforce my healthy decisions
without blame or judgment and welcome my
loved ones to do the same.

Self-Care

What is Self-Care?

The first time the term self-care showed up in my life was again at the family retreat. I thought they were talking about things like brushing my teeth or getting my laundry done, but it got way more involved than that.

Self-care is taking time to check in with yourself before reacting. It considers our mental, physical, and emotional well-being and implements boundaries and healthy actions to support them. Self-care is putting ourselves first where we were usually dead last.

Is this selfish? YES!

Should you feel guilty for that? NO!

Remember that this isn't about being a good human being or working towards a peaceful, healthy planet. I'm talking about our habit of taking care of everyone else BUT ourselves. When we are not working on our wellbeing, we are not coming from a place of wellness. We are coming from a place of lack, hurt, and illness. Our bucket is empty. When we don't feel good spiritually, it plays out physically, and then we don't make good decisions because of it.

Helping someone clean their apartment while they stay intoxicated on the couch doesn't feel good— even if the place doesn't smell anymore. But watching them get sober and clean their apartment feels like a major win!

When we start looking out for ourselves, it isn't selfish in a negative way. We have just decided to start feeling better. Letting go of what makes us feel lesser than, not good enough, or controlling is a relief. We get hooked on what feels good, and we choose something fun for ourselves because we want to, regardless of anyone else's thoughts or whether they need us.

Self-care is the selfish realization that we do matter. We have the right to a healthy, happy, prosperous life regardless of whether our loved ones refuse to get help. We have the right to let go of overbearing control so that life can happily surprise us again.

Self-care is about allowing positivity and fun in again. Self-care realizes there is more to life than saving our loved ones from their problems or lessons. Self-care teaches us to find self-confidence and value in our goals and dreams. And people start noticing the change in you too.

The Bucket

There is a saying— you can't pour from an empty cup.

It makes sense. The givers get used to sharing all their attention, energy, and love and don't notice when the reserves are low.

I'm pretty sure my philosophy was to find a bucket when my cup ran out. Kind of like when you overeat and your stomach stretches. You can eat more next time. So yeah, I figured that if what I gave wasn't enough to fix all the people in my life, I would double my efforts. Before long, I used a metaphorical swimming pool to keep everyone else afloat, but that didn't work either!

I was pouring everything I could think of into saving my loved ones from addiction, depression, and mental health disorders. My kids relied on me to be their rock after our lives had become so shaky. At work, I managed the workload of four people, but I accomplished it all. There was zero time or energy to write, see friends, go to movies, or exercise. I satisfied myself by thinking of all I accomplished at the end of the day before passing out to do it again the next.

Not only was my cup empty, but I was a frazzled unwell little puppy. Stress was chewing me up, and exhaustion was threatening to lay me out flat. I snapped at people without realizing it. Extra demands from coworkers or family proved too much for me to take on, and it wasn't fair to anybody. I used this position to justify my anger and resentment towards my loved ones. I wanted out of this miserable cycle but didn't have a clue how.

When one of my closest friends started speaking to me about filling my cup first, I had to admit that it made sense. I certainly felt empty. So I began attending meditation classes and getting energy treatments. For that hour, I didn't have a single demand of my time or energy. No one could phone or text me. And it was blissfully quiet. I experienced a little slice of peace for the first time, and I was greedy for it. So I began to meditate at home, writing in my journal and shifting negative thought patterns.

I was finally separate from everything else and just being me. It gave me back some perspective, just enough to see through the keyhole and see how I could still love my people without gripping life so tightly.

It made a massive difference for me. It was the room I needed to connect with the Universe and my Inner Being again. I allowed little things to delight me, like the magpies chattering at each other in a tree or the shapes of the clouds. My awareness started to return, and I felt myself healing, bit by bit. My cup was beginning to fill.

In your journal, write out the following:

- **Write out what it feels like to have an empty cup.**
- **Write out how it felt to continue giving your energy when it was empty.**
- **Write out what it feels like to have your cup full.**
- **Write out how it feels to give your energy when it is full.**

By looking at your feelings around your giving/caretaking tendencies, you will recognize when something feels like it is draining your energy or fulfilling you. We got used to feeling bad and then trying to fix the problem that caused it, but that is where we got sucked in. We poured from a negative place. When we build up our foundation of feeling well, we allow healthy giving without sapping ourselves. We are pouring from a positive place, with abundance.

It's time to have some fun. You get to choose anything and everything that feels good but is only for you. No caretaking allowed. You are taking care of yourself without guilt or apologies. Think of the things that you love that have nothing to do with anyone else. What enriches your soul? What do you dream about doing? What makes you belly laugh?

For example, walking/hiking in nature, the ocean, mountains, journaling, going to a concert, yoga, meditation, gardening, singing, travel, and dancing cockatoos fill my cup. I get giddy and excited. I laugh. I feel the beauty surrounding me and remember I am a bright light in the Universe.

Now you try.

- **Write down five things that fill your cup.**
- **Why do they make you feel better?**
- **How often are you doing these things? Can you do them more?**
- **Write down five more.**
- **Write down five things that would fill your cup that you haven't tried yet.**
- **Write down the reasons you haven't tried them.**

Doesn't that feel good? The little person we once were, the dreamer and believer, just jumped for joy at the idea of doing that again. Addiction is scary, and it's hard to remember our dreams when living in a nightmare. But when we shine the light into the shadows, the darkness begins to lift, and we have a new perspective. The more we practice filling our cup, the happier we become and the brighter our light shines. The dark can't exist that way— it's impossible!

It's a beautiful thing when we begin to thrive again. We see the difference now; empty was no fun. Life may have some challenges, but they seem much easier to handle when our cups are full. We can manage with a smile where before, we lashed out. When we feel a little overwhelmed, we can step back and do some self-care techniques to get re-centered. Our lives are more balanced, and life feels like rolling hills rather than a raging roller coaster.

Now that you have this exciting new list to explore, you can begin absorbing all the beautiful things life has to offer. You have these nourishing moments to turn to when you find your loved one's addiction difficult, and you need detachment. You have a new enriching routine that provides joy while upholding boundaries and making challenging decisions. You will gain strength and inner knowledge in your journey to feeling some relief finally. And you can process your feelings more now than you ever have before.

The Power in a Positive Mindset

How we talk has more power than we realize. We talk to our kids, pets, spouses, neighbors, customers, friends, and even ourselves. Do you notice how positively or negatively you tend to speak? The tone we set is what we ask for in our interactions with others and our day. I noticed that the more I bitched and whined, the worse I felt, with everything becoming more challenging. Conversely, the more I was grateful or enjoyed my life, the better and lighter I felt. It took quite a while to discover this self-defeating habit for myself.

After a while, I realized that while I was changing how I spoke outwardly to others, I also needed to change how I talked to myself. My body and Inner Being happened to be listening, so I wasn't keen to continue bashing the divine being that is me.

But where did I learn to do this in the first place?

So much of what we heard growing up sticks in our minds, and it carries into our lives with untold power until one day, we realize that that wasn't our truth but someone else's perception of us at the time. Based on other people's circumstances, we mistakenly repeat their negativity towards ourselves with anger, grief, guilt, shame, hesitation, and fear. Heck, we have entire conversations at lightning speed over what we happen to be eating at that moment, and it is not often a loving appreciation for how our food is about to benefit our body.

I have carried 'I am not good enough' with me my whole life.

It took a lot of self-examination to discover a serious flaw in my approach to happiness. I bought into the criticism, the hurtful comments made in my teenage years, the lack of believing in my dreams, and the feeling I didn't have common sense when making decisions. Dreams were for little kids, not reality. I bought into others' needs being more important than my own because anything else was selfish. I said yes when I wanted to say no.

Although, I would often pick up on a manipulative tactic or comment, and whew— did the brakes go on! There was no budging Jenny when games were afoot. It was a conflict between my need to say no and not wanting to feel bad for saying it. So I came out thinking of myself as small, not enough yet wanting more, with no idea how to achieve that.

I've held myself captive in this idea for too long. My negative thoughts about who I was and what I could create for myself attracted people and experiences that matched this vibe. I could say, "See! I told you so!" about my thinking.

I let fear limit what I was even willing to try. "I couldn't do that. I'm not good enough."

I saw former First Lady Michelle Obama at a speaking event, and something she said stuck with me. She said that as girls and women, we are held to an idea of such a high standard of perfection that when it comes to trying something, we won't even try to step foot on the proverbial 'ladder' for fear of failure. We won't risk anything unless we are guaranteed success. For men, failure is a given, and they are just supposed to get up and start again. It's accepted. She encouraged the women in the audience to get that first toe on the rung, fail, try again, and keep climbing. And to encourage the young women in our lives to do the same. YES!

All the negative crap I had been telling myself for over twenty-five years had held me back. It wasn't serving me. Finally, I recognized it and began redirecting my inner dialogue.

Let's look at a few examples of what we may typically say to ourselves that create limiting beliefs.

1. I can't look for another job because I don't have time to uproot my life.

2. I have to stay home and look after Joe, so he doesn't drink himself to death.

3. I don't have the time to go to counseling/meetings/meditation/yoga.

4. I hate the weight I am at right now.

5. I will never lose weight, get the job I want, stop smoking, etc., so why try?

6. I don't have enough energy to fight with them anymore.

7. This is the way it will always be, and I might as well accept it now.

8. I'll take what I can get.

9. I am not smart enough to figure this out.

10. I fucking hate (insert anything you have said about yourself or someone else here)

It could go on and on, but honestly, this makes me feel awful just writing them. However, this is precisely the revelation I came to and decided it wasn't worth feeling that way any longer.

Grab your journal, rip out one or two pages (I hope you don't need two), and get ready to release all the negative crap that you believed up until now.

1. Write out all the negative critiques you heard about yourself.

2. Do you believe them to be true? How has this affected your life?

3. How do they make you feel about yourself?

4. Write out all the negative self-talk you say to yourself.

5. Where do these ideas stem from?

6. How do they make you feel about yourself?

7. Are the critiques from others related to how you talk to yourself? Why?

Take a good look at your list. It is what you have been feeding your mind. It doesn't look too pretty— does it? Do you have a hard time accepting a compliment without replying in a self-deprecating way? It isn't fair to that little person inside you who wants to be loved.

Right this second, it is time to forgive yourself for allowing this lousy habit to feed your negative self-image, lack of confidence, and any resulting uncertainty in your life. You deserve better, and frankly, no one else will treat you better than you. So it is time to rebuild the self-image you deserve to have.

Anyone who doesn't treat you well after you start changing your mindset will either take note and make some changes or find their way out of your life. You will find that your tolerance for them is pretty low too. You stand up for yourself more, appreciate the genuine people in your life, and your interests become more positively focused.

Let's turn those example statements around in a more self-loving kind of way.

1. I love and accept myself just as I am while I strive towards my health goal.

2. I allow and welcome all opportunities that come my way and know that the Universe will support me.

3. I can move freely about my day, knowing that Joe's addiction is not my addiction.

4. I leave all excuses behind and allow myself the time to take care of my own needs in whatever way I see fit.

5. I reserve my energy for my highest good and people who want to participate in that with me.

6. I know that life is in constant motion, and like a tree, I can move with the wind without breaking.

7. I can have my own needs and wants to be met in my relationship without sacrificing my happiness for the needs and wants of others.

8. If I take a break, I bet I will find a new angle that I haven't thought of before.

9. I love and accept (insert anything you have said about yourself or someone else here) with unconditional love.

Now it is your turn.

1. For every negative statement you made earlier, write a positive affirmation for it.

2. Was this exercise challenging for you? Why?

3. How do these positive affirmations feel now?

4. Once finished, throw away the negative statement sheets. Toss them over your shoulder. Stomp on them. Burn them if you like.

The most important thing that I discovered was that I now had the self-confidence that wasn't there before. Not only was it relevant to my health and wellbeing, but it also became one of the deciding factors in my recovery. I was no longer mired down in self-doubt with the inability to make decisions for myself. While it took some profound life changes to get back on track fully, I wasn't scared by them anymore. It was a massive change to my outlook, but it was exciting to know what I accomplished through some of the most grueling experiences in my life.

By stepping outside my experiences, I could look for the lessons the Universe was trying to teach me without trying to define it as good or bad. As a result, my vision had gone from begrudging everything to realizing a more profound purpose.

I learned how to love someone without owning their journey. I can offer healing support when my bucket is full and re-align myself with my endeavors. It started with giving myself the space to hear what was going on internally and what messages the Universe had been waiting so patiently to deliver.

Who I AM

In recognizing that there was no more room for self-defeating comments in my head, I began to have a different conversation with myself. I had to use positive affirmations and take note of any sneaky doubts that were lingering.

When I first added the following exercise to my self-care routine, it felt a bit uncomfortable. It felt a bit like boasting, and that has never been in my wheelhouse. Yet boasting is about being 'better than' rather than self-assuredness about our abilities.

I soon discovered that saying I AM (fill in a positive statement) about myself felt good— really good. It felt like, "Yeah! I am that!" It gets into those dark places of self-doubt and starts spreading light around until you are glowing.

I started with statements I already knew about myself. Then quickly realized that if I added the experiences I wanted to feel, I would soon know that about myself too. So I expanded my thoughts of who I AM with my goals, and soon I had a list so long that it was fun to realize I had run out of words. Look at all the things I AM!

It takes practice and awareness to catch your train of thought and turn it back into a positive perspective. There are days where I've had a beautiful meditation, practiced my I AM statements, grounded myself, and felt good. Then suddenly, I got thrown into a wild array of emotions because of addiction. It can be challenging to stay present in a challenging moment and not own other peoples' negativity, denial, or unhealthy life choices. But, I also know that the more I use my I AM statements, the more confident I am in myself to handle what may come my way.

The following are examples of I AM statements. There are no rules, and as you can see by my examples, it was a liberating experience to free flow. Use my list as a guide but make a point to sit down and write out your key statements for yourself. Be playful with it; it is meant to be fun.

I AM JOY	I AM IN TOUCH
I AM EMPATHETIC	I AM GENEROUS
I AM SUCCESSFUL	I AM FLEXIBLE
I AM RECEIVING	I AM RELAXED
I AM UNIQUE	I AM SURROUNDED
I AM ABUNDANT	I AM ENCOURAGED
I AM DIVINE	I AM RADIANT
I AM LOVE	I AM INTUITIVE
I AM FORTUNATE	I AM CREATIVE
I AM CONNECTED	I AM WORTHY
I AM GIVING	I AM GENTLE
I AM MUSICAL	I AM SMART
I AM COURAGEOUS	I AM DETERMINED
I AM UNDERSTANDING	I AM SIGNIFICANT
I AM HEALING	I AM GRATEFUL
I AM STRONG	I AM HAPPY
I AM EMPATHIC	I AM ENOUGH

Just writing these out makes me feel like my soul is blooming light and love out into the world! I simply and profoundly AM. I get to choose what I am, and you get to choose what you are. This is where you decorate the walls of your Inner Being with all you know to be true about yourself. All the detachment and boundary exercises were so that you could come to this place and see who you truly are.

You forgot. Life does that. But that little kid inside of you knew all these things once. So it's time to get back to marveling at life with all its adventures.

You know this now because when you travel through the I AM statements, your energy comes alive, your pulse quickens and pumps it through your veins, making you feel happy. But, you also know when you have diminished yourself because you get a sinking feeling like you got punched in the gut. Except you were the one doing the punching!

When you feel negative energy or situations, you can turn to your power statement to re-center yourself. Place your hand over your heart, close your eyes, plant your feet on the ground and breathe in deeply through your nose to I AM SAFE and breathe all the way out through your mouth to I AM GRATEFUL. You can say it aloud or to yourself, but repeat it three to five times or until you feel grounded and secure again.

So, who are you? What do you know yourself to be or even want to be? What are your I AM statements? You can create anything in your life simply by infusing the words with your energy, and every cell in your body will react. How wonderful is that?

Mindfulness

Being mindful is first and foremost noticing what has your attention. Are you focused on stressful things or something you find joyful? What gets your attention? Is it the tragedy on the news? Is it the latest fashion trends or what your favorite celebrity is doing on their Instagram post? Is it loving the sound of your cat purring while he's wrapped around your head?

I have often stopped the car and pulled the kids out on a clear night. We took in the vastness of the stars, the galaxies, the beauty of the moon, all of it. It is the quickest way for me to plugin and to soak up the beauty of the miracle overhead. I become aware that I belong to and am a part of all that magic. I am magical. Tiny sparks of awareness go off, sending messages to all the cells in my body that I AM perfectly loved and held in awe. It is a glorious feeling that I crave when I find myself distracted by obstacles.

Mindfulness, awareness, appreciation: they are all the acts of focusing outside of your worries and troubles and just seeing something for what it is, in that moment, without judgment.

Mindfulness is the pause.

Here is an example.

It was one of those mornings where a light frost had formed on my windshield. As I got into my car, I noticed that my driver-side window had a beautiful pattern that looked like little snowflakes had skated down and across it, leaving star patterns to expand and form, and finally stopping with tiny clusters of crystals. It was like having a two-dimensional chandelier on my window. I could have been lost in the shuffle, trying to get the kids out the door in a timely fashion, and annoyed that I had to use my trusty scraper. Instead, I got in, started my car, and just took in nature's artwork, examining how the light highlighted the shapes and feeling blissed out. I made a point of not scraping my driver-side window and did the rest, feeling a little like I had won a secret game the Universe gave me to play. I smiled instead of grumbling, I noticed the chickadees chirping to each other in the branches overhead, and my kids wondered why I was laughing more than necessary. All was good. Nothing was getting in my wheelhouse that morning.

Being a new parent is a perfect example of when we were mindful and didn't even know it. Examining every little fingernail, curl of hair, and soft sigh is tapping into a pure bliss moment and nothing else. Babies make it easy to do that. We are also pretty mindful when they've pooped their diapers because the moment you aren't mindful can turn into a non-blissful messy clean-up.

It takes some practice to notice your feelings rather than just reacting to the issue at hand. Being mindful enough to consider your emotions before you act is the first step. For example, when I was overwhelmed, I would add the guilt and stress of not coping well when I reacted instead of examining my feelings or caving on a boundary. As soon as I started practicing a slower thinking approach,

I found that the tension wasn't as palpable, and I could manage one thing at a time. I could prioritize my energy and even say no for a change.

After I got the hang of being less reactionary, I noticed that I forgave myself for my slips more and just brought my awareness back to how I wanted to handle myself. As a result, my temper improved with my kids, I listened more, and solutions came easier.

I also stopped cooking stories in my head. I call this 'stinking thinking.' It is not hard to make assumptions in general, and we get a gold star when it comes to addiction. We react to the story we imagine before it even happens, often causing more upset and stress. Our feelings get hurt before anyone says anything. We decide the other person is lying to us before we've got all the information, and we punish them for it too. It defeats the purpose of detachment or healing ourselves.

Slowly but surely, we catch ourselves living outside the reality of the moment we are in presently. We can't go backward because that will bring back some unpleasant feelings. We can't know everything that will happen tomorrow either.

We have today. Today is our gift. It is fresh, and there are opportunities here.

Mindfulness is a practice that allows you peace when you get the hang of it. If you are only concerned about what is in front of you, you can't worry about tomorrow. Or the day after. You can't be at home, at work, and in Hawaii at the same time.

All the time you spent worrying about everything was a distraction and the opposite of mindfulness. It takes a lot of energy to do that continual workout. Also, if we aren't mindful, we can't let go of all the drunken or stoned memories. We can't see them for where our loved ones are today, and if they just came home from treatment and got sober, your constant reminders could be a trigger for them.

In any relationship, there is me, you, and us. So you have to work on yourself, your loved one works on themselves, and you both work on us. With recovery, it may not be easy to have patience while your loved one works on themselves because, let's face it, you've already been waiting a long time. Plus, they are fragile as they reintegrate with work and family life. So our loved ones have to be mindful not to overwhelm themselves by going too fast. Mindfulness gives you that space to release expectations to make room for repair when everyone is stable and ready.

You guessed it; it's time to investigate your struggles with mindfulness and design a new strategy.

In your journal, answer the following:

- **Make a list of everything that you worry about, large or small.**
- **How often do I think about the past? How does this make me feel?**
- **How often do I think about the future? How does this make me feel?**
- **How much worrying do I do every day? Why?**
- **How often do I think about just the moment, hour, or present-day? How does that make me feel?**
- **Where do I struggle the most, and why?**
- **Where do I succeed the most, and why?**
- **If I concentrate on the moment, hour, or present-day, what will happen?**
- **If I focus on the past/future, what will happen?**

These questions set new realizations in motion for you. Addiction wasn't the only thing we were fretting over. Careers, parenthood, family, finances, goals, health— you name it, we have lost our minds over it. Maybe now you see how much emotional and mental time you dedicated to pointless worrying. Maybe you can see where the ulcer originated. Maybe you can see why you are complaining about your life all the time.

When we catch ourselves in this thinking pattern, what do we do? Our problems are significant or even stressful. So how do you manage your life if you aren't thinking about it? Don't we have to keep a sharp eye out for more red flags?

Well, you multiply what you put your focus on, darling. So, if you continue to keep a watchful eye out for every hint of drinking/using, I'm sure you will find it whether it's there or not. If you are there to work on this issue with them, not owning it, mind you— then you must be working in the present with them.

You can only deal with what is in front of you at any given moment using all the healthy tools you have just learned. The handier you get with detachment, boundaries, and self-care, the more you believe in this concept. Don't worry; you will get there. No one is expecting perfection anyhow.

When you need to bring your focus back into the here and now, use the following affirmation to help get you there:

I recognize my past for all it has taught me,
and I am grateful to be where I am today.
I know that my future holds many
opportunities to learn and grow.
I am exactly where I am supposed to be right
now.
The Universe has a divine plan for me, and
everything is designed for my greatest
purpose.
I allow my loved ones to follow their unique
path while I continue to follow mine.
Today is a gift with new possibilities.
I welcome them all and stay focused in the

moment with appreciation.

I AM loved. I AM safe. I AM learning. I AM

present.

This affirmation refocuses away from your past or what you imagine will be in your future. It turns our worry and fear into gratitude and awareness. All hell could be breaking loose, but your new radar senses that a timeout is needed. You take some space, determine what is yours and what is not. You gain a little clarity while catching your breath, deeply in through your nose and out through your mouth. You use this affirmation to remind yourself that no matter what happens, this is happening for you, not to you.

It is happening for your loved ones, not to them. They may have some brutal wake-up calls playing out in front of you, but this is not your journey, nor is it your call to interfere with their learning process. It takes some profound control. Sometimes we need to create a safe space in our minds to re-balance ourselves before we act or make decisions.

Mindful Visualizations

Mindful visualizations are safe places that we create either from our imagination or from experiences we've had. They include the five senses of sight, smell, taste, sound, and touch in great detail. When you begin your visualization, you will know where you are and what it is like down to the tiniest detail. Nothing can change the landscape or how it feels as you have created it. No illness, addiction, or behavior can penetrate this safe space, and it is solely yours.

The idea isn't to lose ourselves in fantasy but rather calm the mind so that we get the chance to regroup. Meditation does this as well but goes much deeper. Mindful visualization is good practice for quietening the mind for meditation and works in situations where you need to quickly bring yourself back to the center— like at work or when you feel triggered.

In your journal, describe in detail your Sacred Space for mindful visualization.

It is your Sacred Space where you feel the wonder of the Earth, the abundance of Mother Nature, and the connection to the Universe. You can use your favorite camping spot, the hidden fort you had as a child or your favorite tree. You can choose a theme such as peace, gratitude, or love for this space, and in the future, you can change this up to fit whatever you need at the moment. Once you have written it out, ensure you won't be interrupted and get comfortable. Close your eyes and visualize your Sacred Space with all your senses. Take fifteen minutes for yourself to relish it and bring your theme to mind. Once finished, write out how this made you feel.

I have included an example to help you.

JOY

I am standing in a field of white where the sky meets the horizon and disappears— no beginning, no end. I am surrounded by a cloud with my scarf loosely wrapped around my neck. I've tucked it into the warmth of my coat. I have fluffy red mittens keeping my hands toasty as I turn my face to the sky. There is a subtle glow of sunlight through the air, and I notice it started to snow. Putting out my hand, I begin to catch delicate little stars, perfect crystalline miracles in contrast to the red yarn. Some are larger and some the tiniest spec of a snowflake, but equally as magnificent in shape. Some have clustered together and become their own little star cloud floating gently to my mitten before melting from the heat of my hand. I am surrounded by miracles, floating about my head, landing on my eyelashes, and leaving little wet touches to my lips. I am a girl living in a snow globe with the Universe, both vast and small, crafting this moment just for me. I AM grateful. I AM blessed. I AM loved. I AM supported. I AM safe.

Every time I think of this, I am reminded of what life is really about and see if I'm on the right track. My Sacred Space is the space I hold for myself to heal. Nothing can penetrate it. I have held space for others, too, keeping the positive energy vibes rocking with the volume up high when my loved one was unconscious in the hospital. I still do when the situation revolves around healthy boundaries. But my Sacred Space is where I am genuinely me again and can experience joy when life threatens to rob it from me.

Being in my Sacred Space almost makes me giddy with delight. I am a kid again, and life is beautiful. I want to take it all in, and the great part is that I can go there whenever I want to.

When I return to the present, I feel calm, less rattled, and prioritize the issues at hand. Anxiety doesn't rule my world anymore, so I react from a place of detached compassion. I recognize the true spirit of my loved ones again, whether they are well or not, and I can plant the seed so they can maybe create Sacred Space for themselves when they are ready and ask for it, of course.

When you were in your Sacred Space, were you thinking of the laundry you had to fold? The bills you needed to pay or the weight that appeared on the scale this morning? No, you weren't. Instead, you were in that moment as the image formed in your mind, and the experience you just had is now part of your day. So you can be mindful on the way to your car, as you cut vegetables for dinner, or take a walk with your best furry friend, enjoying the colors and smells as you go.

You are just being in that moment. But then, you notice the story playing out around you. Where you once were distracted by your cooked-up stories, you now see things just as they are!

A ladybug is just doing ladybug things. That little fish was just doing fishy little things. That whale is just doing big whaley things. There is no judgment about their actions, no preconceived notions on how things should be. Instead, they go about their day with a moment-by-moment action plan of the most uncomplicated design.

Life can be fabulous again. You are worth it! You've endured enough, suffered enough, followed misguided intentions enough. Finally, you are ready to fill your cup with positivity and your new I AM self-awareness. You understand the power of your thoughts and where they can take you. You are relieved to have a Sacred Space of your choosing readily available whenever you need it. And now, you are ready to explore meditation to deepen your connection with your Inner Being and find greater peace.

Meditation

Meditation has played an integral part in my ability to cope, heal, and know myself. I've journeyed within to find my peace and my much-longed-for connection to the Universe.

I'm not going to lie. There are some days where I just could not get past the itch of my clothes' fabric, my breathing feels forced, and I'm not relaxed. But I've learned the act of sitting alone and relaxing was better than taking care of anyone else for those precious minutes. So setting that me-time aside was the point. It was what got me focusing on my self-care and mental state.

Maybe some of you are familiar with meditation, so you are more practiced in the process. For others, this might seem a little whoo-hoo for you. That's okay. It's not as out there as you might think. You can try several kinds of meditation, including guided meditation, breathwork meditation, meditation to music, sound bath meditation, or meditation in silence. I suggest you investigate local meditation groups where you can start with some instruction. There are also many meditation guides on the market if you prefer to learn with a book.

One of the first meditations I went to was a sound bath. I found it perfect because I could lay there and just wonder at the cacophony of different sounds bouncing around the room. I allowed myself to experience the vibrations that the various instruments created in my body. I didn't give addiction, my loved ones, work, or heartache a second thought, just for that hour. It went by remarkably fast, and I was surprised when my awareness went from a sort of expanded thought back into my body.

I loved it! I was hooked! I went in thinking, "Hey, this could be fun for my self-care." But, instead, I came out realizing that this was finally going to get back to my inner child. I discovered who I AM that night, with gongs and rain sticks enchanting my ears. I finally could begin getting back to doing what I wanted without an apology to anyone.

How to Meditate

Mindfulness also comes into play when you are meditating. Geared to think, our brains form thoughts faster than we are even aware. When you have a lot going on in your life, like issues around addiction, it is difficult to plop your butt down on a meditation pillow and focus on your breathing while your mind goes blank. It is like watching that video of gazelles leaping over tourist vehicles while cheetahs are chasing them, all bursting from the shrubbery. Once you think you've settled down, the damn gazelles are racing the other way, and now one has leaped in your car with a cheetah right behind it!

Creating a comfortable space is key. Layer up comfortable mats or sheepskin for your legs. Get a meditation pillow in your favorite color and clear a corner where you can feel peaceful. Maybe you find some beautiful soft music that just lets your mind and body relax. Make it a dreamy space full of love with nothing to take care of, and in this space, the Universe is carrying you. The load is lighter when you step into it. Be free here.

When you first start meditating, don't be too surprised if the dam breaks. Emotions that you have been avoiding can appear, images of your loved one in various states cross your mind, and they can get uncomfortable. That's okay. Let the images come and go— a gentle hello and goodbye rather than a visit. You have designed this space and time to be accessible for healing and allowing the Universe, God, Angels, Spirit, or Source to guide you.

This clearing process starts making room for new revelations, which allows you to hear your Inner Being more. It is a way to know yourself where you went missing before. By allowing your body to relax, your mind can expand into the abundance of loving energy you seek. Meditation is simply the act of quietening and allowing your mind to settle in a peaceful, safe place called the void.

Welcome the void where you are aware but also don't feel like you are in your body. If free-floating is a little tricky at first, do your I AM statements, setting the intention that you are open to receiving self-appreciation with the Universe's support. Then, use your Sacred Space to move you into your meditation. Settle into your deep breathing and let your mind gently soften into peace and love. Repeat a short affirmation, returning to it when your mind wanders. Nothing else is required of you now, no obligations, no chores, no work, no kids, no thoughts of anyone else but you. It is the gift you give to yourself every day, maybe twice a day.

Here are a few beginner tips for you:

Start with a five-minute goal to just sit in your space and let all your muscles relax. Then, as you get the hang of it, set new goals based on how long you think you can go without interruption.

Don't set a timer as it is startling. Instead, turn your phone off and eliminate all possible interruptions. Pets are not invited. They don't need to purr or whine at you right now.

Begin with nice deep breaths in through your nose and release them through your mouth. Let the air in deeply, then out slowly and calmly until your lungs empty. Don't judge yourself on how well you do or whether you are having a little trouble when you first start. Baby steps, baby! It will come.

Try an I AM mantra if you are having more trouble with thought invasion than usual. Keep coming back to I AM_____.

Sitting helps keep you in meditation mode rather than snoring mode. Laying down can work, but people tend to nod off. Do what works best for you. If you have a sore body, use lumbar pillows to support your back and lean against the headboard of your bed or the side of your sofa.

Use your favorite aromatherapy, preferably a pure essential oil, to scent the room and train your brain that that scent means it's time to clear out your mental debris. Then, meditate with a feel-good crystal in front of you or any item that brings you a positive vibe.

After you feel awareness coming back to your body, place your hands over your heart and feel gratitude, then expand it out towards your loved ones. Make a point of journaling your meditation journey. You will be amazed at how far you have come when you reflect on it later.

Finding the right time of day to meditate is a personal choice. Some like to meditate the moment they wake up, while others prefer night. You can meditate during your lunch hour if that works best for you. On the other hand, it may benefit you to meditate twice a day if you are in a difficult stage with your loved one. The more you can step aside for some self-care time, the better.

Meditation is also good for physical, mental, and emotional health as much as it is spiritual. For example, where negative emotions aggravate the energy in our bodies, meditation soothes them to settle back into rhythm. It helps our entire system rebalance, and we physically feel better. Our nerves settle, allowing anxiety to dissipate and depression to lessen. When our body feels good, our emotions follow and vice versa. Meditation helps get you there.

Reflection

The first steps into self-care can be intimidating when we are used to caring for everyone else. It even feels foreign, like thunder may crash down on our heads at any moment. But then we begin to realize that it feels kind of good! Wait a minute, you mean I am just as important as the person in crisis?

We discovered our self-worth again through the series of self-care exercises. While we have obligations, responsibilities, and challenges, we are invested in our lane rather than taking on our loved ones' too. They have their own lives to manage, and we gladly leave them to it, once and for all.

And when we don't get it right the first time, we take note and try again. But it will likely take a great deal of practice and a little ice cream to pull it all off.

I hope that you are feeling some relief now that you have some guidance on rebuilding your life. I know it took a lot of guts to get this far, and I'm sure that journal has some gut-wrenching stuff in it. But, you walked through fire to get to this point, and you should feel proud of yourself.

Continue to dig deep and show up for yourself every day. Make that commitment for your wellbeing and stick to it. Then, change it up and have some fun! Just keep moving ahead with a full cup and a healing heart.

"Talk to yourself like you talk to someone you love."

Brene Brown

You have some powerful tools at your disposal now. It doesn't mean the addiction won't slap you silly or that your loved one will get the picture. These tools are your lifeline out of choppy waters and are always available when you need them.

Continue to add knowledge, skills, and tools to your arsenal. This book was an initial step to building your strength with compassion and a new perspective.

Inevitably, we will need every tool in our toolbox, and our loved ones will test every skill we have. Triggers are present for The Addicted and The Affected, and no one is perfect.

In the next chapter...

In our final chapter, we discuss the realities of recovery, hard choices, and putting healthy supports in place.

Self Care Affirmation

I AM on the evolutionary journey of my own
making.
I am stronger than ever before and love myself
for who I am.
I spend my energy on what feels good,
enriches my soul, and heals my body.
I AM worth it.
Today, I AM the healthiest version of myself.
I turn my most nurturing instincts inward
where I connect with my Inner Being and the
Universe.
I am excited to explore all that life has to offer.

Chapter Eight

When We Get Tested

It is essential to address the challenging stuff like relapse, triggers, trauma, and stress that will threaten to rock your boat. Let's face it; our loved ones can still be in the worst shape ever or have freshly relapsed. Maybe they have been sober for a year, but you are still struggling with codependent behaviors. Life isn't magically balanced out just because we have started turning our lives around.

It is why you have done all this work. You needed new coping skills that you could use instead of spiraling off the deep end when the shit hits the fan. Depending on how ingrained your knee-jerk reaction is to your loved one's addiction, it could take a lot of trial and error before you get the hang of detachment and self-care. That's perfectly okay.

This chapter is tricky because we had more fun focusing on our healing. It is hard to believe that we may still have issues around addiction in the future when all we want is to be free of it all (flight response, anyone?) Unfortunately, without addressing our coping mechanisms and finding self-awareness, we will carry our controlling overcompensating behaviors into new relationships, too.

We can't just ignore the cause and effect that addiction has had on our lives. Our past is part of us. But this book isn't about hiding. Instead, we moved through denial, judgment, and our feelings so that we could process them with awareness. We learned new coping skills that finally allowed joy back into our lives. But, we didn't do all of that and come this far, just to go backward.

Nope. We are survivors. We are done feeling like a victim, and we've grown too much to buy into that mindset again.

The best way to be prepared is to understand where we struggle and create a plan to counter it. Having compassion for our future selves helps us know that no matter what, we will use our new skills to navigate any situation we face, and we will do our best. Knowing this, we can see that our lives won't feel like they did before.

Understanding Triggers

When it correlates to behaviors or feelings around addiction, the definition of 'triggered' is 'to become active; activate.'

Because of the addiction yo-yo, our brains acclimated to react physically and emotionally to any sign of trouble. It can happen when any of our five senses pick up on the red flags from our loved one's using days, even when subtle.

Any number of scenarios can set off a trigger of shock, fear, grief, anger, and even guilt. Either we freak out, run for it, pretend like it didn't happen, or disappear from sight. Not knowing how to handle the instant adrenaline crash causes stress, anxiety, tension headaches, stomach, and digestive issues. Yet, we are still more worried for our loved ones than we are for ourselves.

The cycle repeats itself with every misstep they take, and we follow. The tight ball in our chest gets tighter and tighter until something blows, either our temper or our blood pressure.

Our triggers don't mean that it is a truth-revealing moment, though. I freely admit my thoughts immediately went to the worst-case scenario when there was an innocent and straightforward explanation for my loved ones' actions. So, not everything was related to their addiction, as I thought. Sound familiar?

It is easy to jump to conclusions when money is missing from your wallet or your loved one goes out with friends. But, in reality, you forgot the kids needed lunch money, and in truth, your husband's lunch date is healthy.

It can take time to reverse our immediate reaction, both physically and emotionally— perhaps years. The idea behind self-care and detachment is to get our finger off the trigger and remember another way. Then, one day, you will notice that it doesn't happen as often, or you will react by not reacting for the first time. Then, you will finally feel the results of your self-care practice to realize that there is hope truly.

Examining the complexity of our triggers will reduce the fear involved with them. The guided action plan you create for yourself is your insurance policy for triggers while still staying in the present moment. If our loved one needs an action plan designed around triggers, so do we.

Bang! The Trigger Goes Off

The neighbor called the cops after seeing your spouse intoxicated and driving away from a bar. They show up to the family reunion with a friend they used to use with. There is a bottle hidden in the washing machine when you go to do laundry. Your mortgage payment is gone, and they won't answer their phone. After three years of sobriety, they binge-drink their way to forgetting their best friend died in an accident. You discover they have been lying about work, where they've been, or who they saw.

We could name any number of scenarios that set us off in the past. We don't know when or why it may happen in the future. But there it is, like a gunshot— BANG!! The chain reaction is underway.

In our mind, we are trying to get back to the moments before the trigger when everything was okay. Life was better then, and in one second, it's gone. Adrenaline is pumping our common sense away. When I didn't know how to center myself, I would misdirect my feelings onto other people over the simplest things. I'd lose my mind over the bottle I just found but instead was impatient with the lady trying to ring through my coffee.

I stay in this state of flux until I recognize that I am reacting to an issue that requires boundaries and space. I need my breathing techniques and mindfulness tools now more than ever.

I know I'm strong, intelligent, capable, loving, and quite funny! But, how I go from that stable person to an overwhelmed crazy woman is shocking and quite unsatisfactory to my way of thinking. I couldn't handle the overload of emotions, and I didn't know what to do at that moment. I got slammed with adrenaline with hardly any control over myself. I would pace, slam doors, leave, come back or drive away. Heaven help anyone who tried to go near me when I was like that.

The truth is, the answers can't even get through while we are in this state. We are in flight or fight mode and not really fit for public consumption. So until our adrenaline subsides and we take some space to practice our self-care steps, we are reacting purely on a physical level.

When we are in the beginning stages of our trigger and need to calm down from a panic attack, we need to perform a little CPR on ourselves.

When triggered, I have found the following tips to be very helpful:

1. Focusing on your breath, blow out HARD, then slowly breathe in through your nose to blow out hard again.

2. Repeat three or four times until you feel like you can breathe normally.

3. Place your hands over your heart and repeat: I AM safe. I AM peace. I AM calm. Allow your breath to slow naturally, feeling your heart slow under your hand.

4. Detach from the person, situation, or place. Visualize yourself on a mountain top, free from stress with only the trees and clouds around you. Put what triggered you on the top of the next mountain over. From this vantage point, it looks smaller, less intense, and you have enough space to see your next course of action.

5. Physically remove yourself, find a quiet place where you can lock a door like your car. Allow each feeling to come forward, honor it, say thank you, and let it go. One by one, let them play out as calmly as you can, just letting each move by like a gentle wave in the

ocean. If you need balance, again place your hands over your heart.

6. Massage between your eyes with the tips of your middle fingers, moving to your third eye then towards your hairline. Move your fingers, spreading out in an arc-like pattern, around each temple and softly down your cheeks to meet at your chin. You are drawing a heart on your face. Wear the love right there. It is literally SELF LOVE.

Once I feel a little clearer, I can make my next move. NOW I can think of doing meditation, cleaning the house, or going for a walk. I let the moment pass for now and just refocus my thoughts on how I want to feel. I am careful with my words so that I do not generate negative self-talk. Instead, I use my I AM statements and move what I was experiencing to an objective standpoint. It may take some time, and that's OK.

Looking back, think of a time you were triggered. Maybe it is the worst experience you have gone through. Then, close your eyes and consider what happened leading up to that moment and what transpired after.

In your journal, answer the following:

- **Write out everything that you would consider to be a trigger in your life.**

- **Write one story about the situation that triggered you, including the result.**

- **What was your reaction?**

- **How did it make you feel?**

- **If something similar happened tomorrow, what would you do differently?**

- **Write your action steps to handle your trigger in a healthy way.**

- **What do you think the result would be? How would you feel?**

- **Is this a repeating problem in your life? If so, what changes can you make to break the cycle?**

These days may come again for you. But, beginning with the smallest changes towards your self-care, health, and safety, you will know what is right for you— when it is right for you. There is no right or wrong here; it is all a lesson. When we are in the thick of it with our loved one, or even if it was a horrendous childhood we are recovering from, we can have triggers going off all the time, even when the situation isn't substance-related. But, if all we are doing is reacting like the ball inside the pinball machine, eventually, we will have a breakdown.

Your list of triggers is an objective way to get control back when you thought it was what everyone else was doing to you. When you have become more proficient and balanced, you will know that nothing anyone else does or says matters one bit. You get to choose what you allow in your life, including how you react.

It is also a time to offer yourself some forgiveness. In the past, you were looking for some way to control an unbearable situation. Unfortunately, you didn't have the tools to handle it well. Now, you are starting a new self-care practice, and you won't be an Olympian at it overnight. I continue to work on this every day too.

There could genuinely be a severe anxiety disorder to overcome. That is allowed! You may benefit from the steps in this book but need some extra support from a mental health professional and your doctor. However, knowing that you are in charge of taking care of yourself, you know this may be an essential step in your recovery. So keep going and don't give up.

Jenny Truth: You are not the only one who has triggers. Your loved one experiences them often. It doesn't even have to be something

terrible to set them off. Exciting news or a
happy occasion can create adrenaline, just like
a negative one. If they are still in the cycle of
addiction, they may not recognize the triggers
and turn to their vice instinctively. They have a
long twisty road to identifying them and acting
differently, too. You can't teach this to them,
even with all your handy new information.
They must come to a place where they are
ready to drop their denial and get help on
their own terms.

Decision Making

All these reflection exercises may have made you realize
that you have some significant life changes to make. It can
be an overwhelming idea. But, when I finally came to that
point, I realized that I had been too scared for too long to
move ahead. And now that it was in front of me? While
somewhat shaky, I had a new self-confidence that I could
survive and thrive in my life.

Maybe you need to sleep in a separate room. Maybe
you need a separate bank account. Maybe you need to
move into your own home. Maybe you need to save
money so you can. Maybe you need space in the
relationship to heal for yourself, then decide whether you
are willing to try again. Maybe you have to let your
sister/brother go and live your life. Maybe you are not safe
in the house when your loved one is intoxicated. Maybe
your kids aren't either. Maybe you can overlook your
loved one's addiction, whether they clean up or not, and
be completely satisfied with your life without leaving.

You get to design your life the way YOU want it. You will
get plenty of advice from all the people who think they
have the answer and you'll hear a lot of 'shoulds' when
they are talking to you. They mean well. It is hard for

people who love us to watch us go through so much pain — and you know this experience too well yourself. Their advice may be to dump them, move out, take the kids, ignore them, dangle whatever carrot you can until they get sober.

I bet you've thought these things too. It's more complicated than that, isn't it? It could involve more heartache, loneliness, change, financial burden, or struggle. Our pride may not withstand another blow by having our issues made public with our family or friends. Of course, all of it is fear-based, but that doesn't mean it isn't a powerful element of persuasion. Some of us are more than aware that we need changes in our lives but don't know where to start.

Making a decision starts with awareness of the problem(s), investigation, and bravery to make just one step forward. In your journal, answer the following questions. You can choose to answer all of them or choose a scenario(s) that suits your situation:

Scenario One: Nothing changes and stands as it is right now.

1. What would happen if nothing changed with your loved one?

2. How would you feel?

3. What would happen if nothing changed with you?

4. How would you feel?

5. Is this something you can live with? Why or why not?

6. Are my safety and wellbeing a priority? How?

7. What is the worst-case scenario if nothing changes?

8. What is the best-case scenario if nothing changes?

9. If you have arrived at any conclusions, write your decision from the perspective of positive self-love.

Scenario Two: Our loved one's addiction is in full swing, and you are working on your own healing.

1. If the cycle of addiction is a part of my life, but my loved one is not willing/able to help themselves, what would that look like?

2. Is it possible for me to stay in this relationship while my loved one is in addiction and continue to heal myself? Why or why not?

3. How would I feel if this was the case?

4. What would be my biggest obstacles?

5. Is it necessary for me to leave this relationship to continue to heal myself? Why or why not?

6. How would I feel if this was the case?

7. What would be my biggest obstacles?

8. If I were to stay, are my safety and wellbeing a priority? How?

9. If I were to leave, are my safety and wellbeing a priority? How?

10. If you have arrived at any conclusions, write your decision from the perspective of positive self-love.

Scenario Three: Our loved one's addiction is part of our life, but we are both working on healing ourselves.

1. If the cycle of addiction was part of my life, but we were each working on healing/sobriety, what would that look like?

2. Does healing my life around the cycle of addiction include my loved one? Why?

3. Am I safe, and is my wellbeing a priority? How?

4. Is it possible for me to heal my life while my loved one is struggling with their sobriety but still trying?

5. How would I feel if they were still a part of my life?

6. What would be my biggest obstacles?

7. How would I feel if they were not a part of my life?

8. What would be my biggest obstacles?

9. If you have arrived at any conclusions, write your decision from the perspective of positive self-love.

Scenario Four: Our loved one's addiction is no longer a part of our life.

1. If the cycle of addiction was no longer part of my life, what would that look like?

2. Does my life without addiction include my loved one? Why?

3. Am I safe and my wellbeing a priority? Why?

4. How would I feel if the cycle of addiction was no longer part of my life and included my loved one?

5. What would need to happen for that to take place?

6. How would I feel if the cycle of addiction was no longer part of my life and did not include my loved one?

7. What would need to happen for that to take place?

8. If you have arrived at any conclusions, write your decision from the perspective of positive self-love.

The idea of doing these exercises is to analyze our feelings as we ponder our options. Of course, our first instinct would be a hard NOPE whenever the idea of a painful decision popped up. Your feelings are your guidance system showing you what feels good or not. We must then base our decisions on the boundaries we determined earlier.

When you are coming from a place of an empty cup, damn near everything feels terrible— that's a sign that you haven't made healthy choices, and it's time to start. When you are coming from a place of a full cup, and something feels off— that's a sign that you can move away from a poor choice. When your cup is full and something feels good— do it!

As you wrote your answers, did you come up against a hard no? Was that reaction based on fear? Or was it based on an honest assessment of what is best for you? A hard no is a sign that you aren't going in that direction. When you aren't sure, it makes sense to question the pros and cons and examine your feelings and reasons for each. Then take note if you feel more confident about one direction over another.

No one is deciding for you; only you can do that. Even when you think you have been trapped in your situation, and believe me, it sucks to realize it, but you choose to be there. What you choose now can be based on a healthy inspection of who you were then and who you are becoming. The decisions you make can be small steps or one giant gutsy leap.

Here's a straightforward way of looking at the decision-making process.

Healthy place/space = healthy decisions. Unhealthy place/space = poor decisions.

Got it?

The Blinders Come Off

If we were in denial about the effect of addiction on our lives, we could also have been in denial about the real person behind it. Of course, there are many factors regarding addiction and codependency, but I think it is time to address a rather important elephant in the room.

You thought you had a princess or a knight in shining armor, complete with a romantic idea about their behavior. Oh, they weren't perfect, but you saw something in them that no one else did. We could forgive our loved ones for pretty much anything, and if we loved each other, it would be okay. Besides, they were always sorry for hurting us. Or worse, maybe they weren't, and we accepted it as something we were doing wrong. Add some marriage vows to complicate the issue legally, and we have a bigger excuse to stay in an unhealthy relationship.

It is a harsh reality to learn the person you love is not a decent human being.

Whether binge drinking with the buddies or snorting cocaine in the lady's washroom, if they were rude, selfish, ignorant, or mean, liquor or drugs will only enhance this personality trait. In addition, some people get physically abusive when they are intoxicated. Without getting too deep into the cycle of abuse, we know our habits around addiction are likely linked to the abusive cycle as well. Our new awareness can bring about some interesting challenges because we probably blamed their addiction for their abusive behavior and forgot they acted that way sober too.

When I say abuse, I don't just mean physical or sexual abuse. It includes mental and verbal abuse.

When your loved one is busy yelling and calling you names, hollering about your responsibility to hold down the household with a full-time job as they hop into the unemployment line for the fifth time that year? Yeah. Insert a mental image of the middle finger, please.

And if you think they will change when they are sober? Sorry honey, you may be in for a rough wake-up call.

They won't change their beliefs and who they are at their core just because the substance has cleared their system. It would take a massive face plant to shake them out of their way of thinking. Or possibly a lengthy stint in a recovery center. Until they are a willing participant, your loved one isn't going to change.

Of course, substance abuse inhibits common sense, respect for laws or boundaries, and increases impulsiveness. But if your loved one was capable of scamming or robbing someone when they were sober, they have even fewer qualms about it when they are drunk or high. They just have bigger and better stories about it until they get caught.

Are your loved ones ready to accept that they are responsible for their stinking mess of opinions, behaviors, and treatment of others? Or is this who they are? Unfortunately, being so rooted in their thought patterns and habits may mean they won't ever change. So you have some decisions to make, one's you have likely been putting off.

If this resonates with you about your situation, then journal your answers to the following questions:

- **Write about your relationship with your loved ones if you think they are abusive.**
- **How does this make you feel?**
- **Write about the times your loved one was manipulative or took advantage of you.**
- **How does this make you feel?**
- **Can you live with a person who hurts you, whether it is physical or not?**
- **Do you believe your loved one genuinely wants to change? Why or why not?**
- **If your loved one came home from treatment and began acting in an abusive manner again, what would you do?**
- **Are you ready to move on from this situation? Why or why not?**
- **Are you ready to get professional help? Why or why not?**

I hope that if you have learned anything from this book so far, it's that you are important. Your happiness isn't just your goal, honey. It's your right. It isn't just time for detachment and boundaries, though that will help get you started. It is time for a safety meeting.

If you are going to go through hell at the hands of your spouse or family member, then you know, deep down, that you can't do that anymore. Not only are you risking your safety, but your kids too. Enough is enough. I AM doesn't make room for "I am okay with getting hit. I am okay with being spoken to like that. I am okay with...."

Please, consider looking into support groups and counseling. Heck, do that whether there is abuse present in your relationship or not. The bigger the support system, the sturdier your foundation. It is an excellent way to fill your cup, even if it scares the pants off you. In addition, there are mental health hotlines, social media groups, and Al-anon chapters in your area to make your healing journey less isolating.

While we have many helpful new tools to pull from and have gained a new love for ourselves, it is also beneficial to know that we aren't alone. Having physical people to turn to, who have been through a similar journey, is a relief when you thought no one could possibly understand.

Calling in Support

No matter what you think, you are not alone. But, unfortunately, the isolation of addiction convinces us that no one can understand what life is like for The Addicted or The Affected. It is a defense mechanism designed to protect ourselves from further upheaval or pain, but that same idea prevents us from opening up to people who can properly support and guide us.

And there is no one scarier than a therapist, counselor, or addiction specialist. (I will refer to them all as addiction specialists to keep it simple)

Because, dear one, these people know precisely what happens behind closed doors, the excuses used to justify our actions, and why we make them. The professionals have seen and heard it all. So, we can't fool them into believing we are okay any more than our loved ones convince people they can control their addiction.

If we can't fool them, then they can see right through us, can't they? The answer is— yes. But that is how we will finally be seen, dear one.

The blessing is their goal isn't to judge or shame you but instead support you through your recovery. That's right— your recovery. Addiction specialists are not just for our loved ones but us too, and The Affected need to go through guided healing just as much as The Addicted do.

But, we often feel kicked to the curb with all the focus on making The Addicted better and steady in recovery. I know I did. Without an invitation to family therapy sessions and information on how we are supported, The Affected get left to figure it out on their own. Add any difficulty or wait periods to getting appointments, and we move farther away from getting the immediate help we so desperately need.

All the mental roadblocks we experience about asking for help are the same ones our loved ones face. The unknown is a far more terrifying place than the comfort zone we are accustomed to, healthy or not.

Hey, some of us will gladly head straight for a therapist's office, and I applaud you if you are one of them. And some of us misguidingly seek therapy as a way to get all the answers to 'fix' our loved ones. Yup, I've been there too.

I can attest that you aren't alone for being intimidated by counseling or feeling like you are about to go on trial. And, with all your work with this book, you know that touching the truth opens wounds barely patched together, and therapy will do the same. But just like this book, your truth will be honored, respected, and gently guided through a series of steps towards recovery and healing.

I am not a trained professional nor try to represent counseling services in any way. Instead, I hoped to introduce a new perspective that helps facilitate your healing journey, and if that includes seeing addiction specialists, this book holds your hand towards that goal.

"How do I know when I need professional help?" you may ask. Here is a list of some indicators:

- You are having suicidal or self-harming thoughts.

- You are having uncontrollable anxiety, panic attacks, or outbursts.

- You are developing obsessive coping mechanisms like overzealous cleaning, organizing, or perfecting.

- You are developing addictive behaviors of your own.

- You are having trouble taking care of yourself, your family, or going to work.

- Your family or friends are unable to understand or support you in a healthy way.

- You are feeling overwhelmed and unable to cope no matter what you try.

- You need a neutral safe place to talk to someone who knows their stuff.

Therapy is not reserved solely for the mentally ill. Mental health is just as important as physical and spiritual health. In fact, it is believed that where the mind goes, the body will travel, which interprets as our physical ailments come from the pattern of our thinking, stress, worry, and unresolved trauma. Louise Hay made her entire career from this concept.

We worked through fear in Chapter 4, along with judgment, shame, and guilt. All of these feelings are normal. The more power we give them, the less connected we are to ourselves and our goal of overall wellness. If we let them, they can prevent us from getting the relief we need through professional mental health services.

In your journal, answer these questions:

- **How do I feel about going to therapy? Why?**
- **Where are these feelings coming from?**
- **What is the worst-case scenario for getting counseling?**
- **What is the best-case scenario for getting counseling?**
- **Is there something physically preventing me from going, like finances or schedule?**
- **What are some of the ways I can make a plan around those issues to ensure I can get the help I need?**
- **Who are the people most likely to help and support me accomplish this goal?**

Looking at our hangups around mental health and therapy shows us how many stops we put on it ourselves and how many are actual barriers to receiving care. But rest assured, there is a solution for every problem.

If you can't afford therapy sessions, double-check your health care insurance and government agencies. There are also many free supports through Al-Anon, therapist's social media accounts, support groups on Facebook, apps, and other books. Visit www.jennykennedy.ca for my suggested reading book list.

Keep this in mind. We easily prioritize spending money on things that feel good and procrastinate paying for things that don't. If you find yourself buying a new pair of shoes you don't need while making excuses that therapy is too expensive, then your priorities need adjusting.

The same can be said for your schedule. Go on your lunch break, ask a friend or family member to watch the kids, heck— take the kids with you if you have to. Evening and weekend appointments may be available. Make the time. Prioritize your mental health.

It takes some major self-care chops to find a way around your roadblocks to going for counseling. Getting help for where you feel weakest is actually the greatest strength of all.

What to Expect in Counseling

There is a process for booking mental health appointments. Government-run offices can have different procedures than private practices, and the office settings can also differ. Heck, they can vary between cities, provinces, states, and countries with governing bodies mandating various policies.

You may book an appointment and, after answering a few questions, see a counselor right away. Or, you may end up going through several steps first.

Some practices are more than just addiction specialists, handling a wide range of mental health issues for all ages. These facilities will likely have a series of intake procedures to determine which department to refer you to. For example, where I'm from, public mental healthcare is free for residents. But not only was there an initial phone call but an intake appointment too. From there, I had to wait for an additional appointment to see a counselor. At the time, I found the number of hurdles extraordinarily frustrating and a deterrent. Then, of course, if someone was in crisis, they directed patients to the hospital for care.

Don't let this prevent you from getting help; instead, expect it may not be a straight line to seeing a therapist. Be patient as you get set up in their system.

If the practice focuses on addiction and family counseling or is a private practice, you may have less hassle getting the help you need. The same intake questions happen with private practices; however, you may get in sooner depending on their schedule.

If you are in a crisis, make sure you communicate that clearly to the staff and receive help immediately.

As with any government-funded facility, the offices tend to be somewhat sterile despite the staff's attempts to make them pleasant. Expect office furniture, desks, and lighting, but with privacy blinds and some of the counselor's personal decorations for color and encouragement. Some therapists will use lamps instead of fluorescent lighting to help you feel more comfortable.

Private practices are still functional with office furniture; however, they tend to be more colorful, welcoming, and softer in approach. As a result, you are more likely to find sofas or chaise loungers, comfy armchairs, and ambient light. Soothing paint colors and draperies help complete the room.

Perhaps your health insurance covers the cost of private counseling, or your health care coverage includes mental health through government programs. If not, you will pay out of pocket for your sessions, and billing can vary. Some therapists offer sliding scale fees based on your income and what you can afford. Others charge an hourly fee that you pay upfront before each session. It is worth asking how they handle their billing during the intake questions while providing your health insurance information.

Regardless of public or private practice, you will be talking to trained therapists who genuinely want their clients to get the help they need. While being an empathetic ear, they will remain neutral as they work with you. They aren't there to be your best friend or the means to let off steam. Instead, your therapist will use constructive questions and listening skills to guide you through the healing process.

It will take building mutual trust, having faith in their methods, and the willingness to try something new for therapy to be successful. Your counselor will listen to you, of course, encouraging you to open up and speak freely. They just won't let you ramble aimlessly.

Therapy is brave— and hard work. So, emotionally, feeling drained for the first few sessions is expected. But, as you begin to see the benefits from counseling, you will start looking forward to your sessions.

Finding the Right Therapist

Getting mental health services can be intimidating and time-consuming. Meeting a counselor when we are vulnerable is no small feat. We are trusting them with our inner sanctum, which happens to be in turmoil.

Maybe this person was referred to you by a family doctor, friend, or perhaps assigned by the intake worker. It can be hard to gauge how well they fit when the playing field isn't even. It isn't like your therapist will share their entire personal life with you, now are they? Trusting people hasn't exactly paid off for you, so why should this?

During your intake, I recommend asking some questions about who you'll be seeing. What are their credentials? How long have they been specializing in addiction? Do they treat The Addicted and The Affected? How long have they been practicing at that location?

Often, people in recovery turn to careers related to addiction to help others based on their personal experience with addiction. Unfortunately, intake workers won't provide that information due to privacy laws; however, your therapist may be open about their past. These people have slain the dragon and are willing to share examples of trouble and success from their life to help establish your trust.

Therapists will be straightforward, honest, and call you out on damaging behaviors. However, they will also be supportive, understanding, and empathetic while doing so. You want that. You aren't there to be patted on the back and sent away. Therapy isn't a bandaid— it is surgery. Healing may take time, but counseling gets deep into the wound to do it.

What if you aren't confident with your therapist after a few sessions?

Two things need to happen.

First, you need to seriously check in with yourself. Are you wholeheartedly participating in your sessions? Are you appeasing them with what they want to hear but not doing the work? It wouldn't be surprising considering your people-pleasing skillset, would it? Are you labeling them as bullies (or another derogatory name) because they make you focus on painful issues? Do they misunderstand you because you haven't been forthcoming or honest?

Second, have you voiced your feelings or confusion to your therapist? It isn't constructive if you aren't actively communicating where you are at with your counselor. How can they possibly know how to switch gears and get back on track? Time to get the big bloomers on and learn how to have adult conversations for the sake of your mental health.

Here's the secret: Your therapist will teach you how!

Not only will they help you learn boundaries and how to have conversations around them, but your therapist will show you how to have healthy relationships, period. Considering everything we've been through, that is worth its weight in GOLD!

But if you aren't jiving with your therapist despite your best efforts, it is time to look elsewhere. Yes, it will feel like starting over. And yes, it makes you feel like throwing in the towel. Just don't give up. It is your healing at stake, and your therapist will understand. They want you to be successful too.

Explain your feelings, thank them for their help, and request a referral to a colleague. Then, if you can stay within the same practice, the counselors can confer on your file, and it won't be quite the same as starting from scratch. Otherwise, you can simply begin researching other addiction specialists in your area. But, again, if you have trouble, Al-Anon will be an excellent source for referrals, even if you aren't attending meetings.

Counseling is more like a ball of yarn than a lovely straight piece of string. It feels messy, frustrating, and like nothing will ever come of it. Until one day, you've knit yourself a colorful, cozy sweater out of that messy ball, and it keeps you warm when it gets cold.

Getting Help for Your Children

You aren't the only one who needs to learn new coping skills. If you have children, they have been witness to not only your loved one's addiction but also your hyper-vigilance trying to manage it.

Unchecked, your kids learn the same skills. Maybe they have been doing their best to help you, to make things easier for you. But, on the other hand, perhaps they are acting out because there are no rules and you have no energy to make them. Maybe they are developing an addiction of their own. And worse, like in my situation, they run away after suffering a complete mental health crisis of their own.

This knowledge could bring a wave of guilt with it. And trust me, I feel you. So know that by reading this book, getting therapy, and starting your healing journey, you also show them how resilient you are and how to move forward healthily. Now, instead of shielding them from addiction, you actively include them in conversations about it and teach them how to manage their feelings.

You are now teaching your kids healthy self-care practices in all forms.

Just as it is tempting to take your loved ones by the ear and shove them into detox, we can mistakenly use the same approach to counseling for our children. When we are at the end of our rope, patience is a long-lost fantasy, but our kids need the reassurance that you are still there for them. Addiction has been robbing them of stability and wellbeing too.

Ask your therapist if they handle youth counseling or have a referral for you. Get their advice on approaching therapy with your kids and have a conversation with your children in a quiet, safe place. It helps to pick a time when they will be calm and can handle a genuine talk. Don't do all the talking, and make sure you hear their concerns or hard feelings because the damn may break. They may tell you things you didn't know they experienced. Things you didn't know they felt. Honor and respect your kids for sharing with you and actively include them in the plan to introduce therapy.

Children are hesitant, just like we are. But, while they may have to go, you can give them a choice on which day, what time, or even what they wear to the appointment. By giving them an option, we provide them with an element of control, so they are more likely to cooperate.

Be prepared, though. Therapy threatens your kids' sense of balance, the unknown proving too much for them to handle. In addition, if you and your kids have experienced trauma, homelessness, financial insecurity, etc., they may see this as a threat rather than a relief. It may take several conversations to introduce them to counseling. But if they are in a mental crisis or at risk of hurting themselves, you cannot delay. If you can't physically get them to a therapist or the ER, you may need the assistance of paramedics or emergency health professionals.

I've been there too, and you have to consider the physical risk to yourself as you seek help for your child. While heartwrenching, your child's wellbeing may be beyond your capabilities at the moment. Be sure to discuss your children's situation thoroughly with your therapist, so you have the proper support as well.

It takes a village to raise a child. Part of your child's support plan needs to include teachers, coaches, doctors, therapists, and other family members to maintain steady messages and a stable foundation. Unfortunately, mixed messages or lack of knowledge could create a lot of confusion for your child, resulting in emotional outbursts, trouble in school, sleep, or appetite issues.

Keeping everyone on the same page takes a great deal of pressure off of you as well. You are no longer constantly managing a difficult situation on your own or making excuses for your child's behavior. School counselors can partner with your child's therapist and doctor too.

There is one thing to note. When your child begins therapy, the counselor often wants to speak to the parents separately from the child, then together as a group after talking to them alone. The counselor needs to be brought up to speed, but you can speak frankly without causing any damage to your child by speaking to them alone first. Then, when it's their turn, your child needs to voice their concerns and tell their story without worrying about a reprimand.

It is tempting to insist on being in the room, and I understand the overwhelming protective instincts we developed around addiction. However, kids learn not to upset or hurt their parent(s) as a coping mechanism, defeating their healing process. Instead, let the counselor earn their trust to speak freely. They, too, need to know how to say no safely, about boundaries, and how to negotiate difficult situations.

Above all else, we don't want them to learn codependent behaviors any more than we want them to learn addictive ones. The path to your child's mental health and healing is another ball of yarn, but you now have a team to help unravel it.

One last thought. As you continue to learn about codependent behaviors, boundaries, etc., it is easy to find yourself confused about where your parenting was successful and where it fell short. Go easy on yourself. You did the best you could, and now that you have some guideposts, you can do better. Kids are resilient and deserving of our praise, and so are we. As we get better, our children do too.

Other Support Systems

Support systems are all around us, should we care to look. Having people to turn to outside the therapist's office is also essential, and not just when we need something.

Our closest, most trusted friends and family are people who not only care about you but want to help you be well and recover. They have your best interests at heart, and while they may not fully understand the layers to addiction or your situation, they support you in healthy ways.

These people have likely been missing you badly.

You may have to explain your boundaries and their importance— especially with well-meaning family members. They are, after all, meant to protect your relationship with others, not obliterate it. People capable of adult conversations full of mutual respect and understanding are worth holding on to, whereas those who blow past your no, disrespect you, or don't align with your new values are people to keep at a healthy distance. The amount of space you keep between you is up to you.

What if you don't have any friends left now?

Isolation is a reality with addiction as much as with abuse— the more attention addiction requires, the less time we have for our other relationships. People have busy lives too, and they prioritize time for people who do the same. It isn't intentional, just a natural progression as we become more and more lost.

Reach out to your old friends, co-workers, and relatives with whom you've lost touch. Don't start the conversation with drama/trauma but ease into it as an explanation for your distance. Then, test the waters to see if you can trust them in your inner circle using your new boundary tools. Reciprocate invitations to meet, push yourself to get out of the house. You don't have to talk about your loved one's addiction or therapy all the time. Instead, find reasons to laugh and get fresh air. Be out in the world!

If rekindling friendships isn't possible, then it's time to make new ones, and a great place to start is with support groups like Al-Anon. Members know exactly where you are coming from and can sponsor you just like AA does for The Addicted. Al-Anon has their version of the Twelve-Step system, should that appeal to you. While they have many meetings at various locations throughout the week, Al-Anon also hosts mingling events for like-minded people to have fun in a safe environment.

Your therapist could suggest group sessions, and while the purpose isn't exactly to make friends, you can continue your group conversation over coffee with a new acquaintance.

Try volunteering at an animal shelter or another organization that makes your heart happy. Guaranteed, you will meet other people with the same interests. Invite your neighbor and their kids over for a BBQ. Tend to your spirituality, whether through church, energy healing, or returning to your cultural heritage.

The more you branch out, the more extensive your support network. Being supported looks like sharing fun activities, holding space for each other, creating together, promoting each other's work, referring opportunities, taking a class... the list goes on. There's nothing selfish about it, even though you gain significantly from it. Instead, having a healthy support network is self-care by sharing your light with others. They get brighter for it, and so do you.

Reflection

It was a rough chapter to get through because we had to look at the tough stuff again. It was necessary to be prepared for ongoing addiction or relationship issues with our loved one, though, wasn't it? If we could bippity-bobbity-boo everything into a blissful existence, we would have done it by now.

Knowing this, we get the chance to flex our self-care muscles and practice everything we learned to create a different outcome than we experienced before. Bit by bit, step by step, we see the solutions for ourselves where before we had no idea.

We explored counseling and how it helps you become a powerhouse in your recovery. While it may still be intimidating, you can consider it in your healing timeline, along with making room for healthy relationships with friends and family. Now, we see that there is more to life than just managing but thriving. We are more than all the superpower micromanaging we did to cope with our loved ones' addiction.

I hope that you feel empowered to manage whatever comes your way. I hope you feel supported to make any tough decisions you have been putting off. I hope that you find a connection with me and others on your self-care path. Finally, I wish you great happiness and joy in your life.

You are on your way... safe from the storm.

Strength Affirmation

I AM grateful for the strength I now have.
I know that when times seem difficult, I can
merely shift my perspective to appreciate the
lesson in the moment.
When I reflect on where I have been, I can see
more clearly where I am going.
I am stronger for the contrast in my life, and I
appreciate the times I am sailing in calmer
waters.
I AM fully supported, and I can simply reach
out to my people and the Universe whenever I
feel the need.

Chapter Nine

Conclusion

Take a good look at the journal you have been using. Flip the pages and look how far you've come. There is a substantial amount of your feelings and thoughts written, isn't there? Congratulations on working through some pretty tough stuff and making yourself a priority.

We had to start by getting our story out on the page. Finally, it feels like a blessed relief and a painful reminder simultaneously. Yet this process validates our journey, so we know what was real and where our perception was off. We see it from the perspective of today, and it is clearer.

It's a revelation with a heavy emotional price. The truth hurts!

The more we went through the exercises, the more we practiced self-care, the less addiction got our attention. It feels good to begin feeling like ourselves again. Our confidence will build along with optimism.

There will be obstacles. Taking a healthy look at our challenges makes us more prepared. As we continue to heal and grow, we can decide what changes to make and where we may not be ready. We know that there is support for people just like us, should we choose to investigate it.

When addiction was at its worst in my life, I didn't know any better than trying my best for my family and loved ones. The toll didn't matter as long as they were safe. I didn't see that the more overwhelmed I got, the more strained it was for my kids. I didn't see know any other way or that I had options. I was deeply invested in my caretaking role until it nearly broke me.

I developed the exercises in this book after first doing them myself. I took what I learned from the family retreat, therapists, counselors, supports, and others like me and did the heartwrenching work to pull my life back on track.

Addiction played a gambit on me, and I followed along. Don't get me wrong; there was love, joy, and laughter in my life too. I am grateful for many blessings, including my loved ones. I know that I will always be learning and growing through my experiences and self-reflection. You will too, but don't stop.

Question your feelings. Think about your reactions. Is there a better way that I didn't think of? Did you try something of mine that wasn't a fit but discovered another approach? Journal it all and share your progress with me.

Just don't give up. Instead, explore your healing with eagerness for a better day, every day towards a better life. Nourish your growth with gentle grace for yourself and your loved ones, even if from a distance.

Thank you for bravely reading this book and doing the tough work of healing. I applaud you, appreciate you, and wish you a loving release from the pain of your loved one's addiction.

Gratitude Affirmation

I AM grateful for all that I have in my life.
I AM blessed to give and receive love between
my friends and family.
I AM guided and supported by the Universe
while I walk my path.
I appreciate the abundance of joy, pleasure,
love, and adventure in my life, and I look
forward to even more.
I AM resilient, strong, and determined in all
that I do.
I AM well and accept all that is for my greatest
good.

Chapter Ten

Reading List

I recommend the following authors and books to further your healing journey with codependency and addiction. Updated frequently, The Reading List will have my latest favorites added as I find new gems worth sharing, so remember to check back.

Please visit www.jennykennedy.ca to purchase.

Gabor Mate

- In the Realm of Hungry Ghosts - Close Encounters with Addiction

Brene Brown

- Daring Greatly
- I Thought it was Just Me
- Dare to Lead
- Braving the Wilderness
- The Gifts of Imperfection

Melody Beattie

- Choices
- Journey to the Heart

- Codependent No More – How to Stop Controlling Others and Start Caring For Yourself
- Codependent No More Workbook
- The Language of Letting Go
- More Language of Letting Go
- Beyond Codependency

Cory Muscara

- Stop Missing Your Life

Terri Cole

- Boundary Boss – The Essential Guide to Talk True, Be Seen, and (Finally) Live Free

Dr. Nicole LePera

- How to Do the Work – Recognize Your Patterns, Heal from Your Past, and Create Yourself

Dr. Alexandra Solomon

- Loving Bravely – 20 Lessons to Self-Discovery to Help You Get the Love You Want
- Taking Sexy Back – How to Own Your Sexuality and Create the Relationships You Want

Louise Hay

- You Can Heal Your Life
- Heal Your Body – The Mental Causes for Physical Illness and the Metaphysical Way to Overcome Them
- The Power is Within You
- Meditations To Heal Your Life
- Love Your Body

Najwa Zebain

- Welcome Home – A Guide to Building a Home for Your Soul

Dr. Joe Dispenza

- Becoming Supernatural – How Common People Are Doing the Uncommon

David Ji

- Sacred Powers – The Five Secrets to Awakening Transformation
- Secrets of Meditation Revised Edition – A Practical Guide to Inner Peace and Transformation

Harriet Lerner, Ph.D.

- The Dance of Anger - A Woman's Guide to Changing the Patterns of Intimate Relationships
- The Dance of Fear - Rising Above Anxiety, Fear, and Shame to Be Your Best and Bravest Self
- The Dance of Intimacy - A Woman's Guide to Courageous Acts of Change in Key Relationships
- The Dance of Deception - A Guide to Authenticity and Truth-Telling in Women's Relationships
- Why Won't You Apologize - Healing Big Betrayals and Everyday Hurts

Chris Prentiss

- Zen and the Art of Happiness

Chapter Eleven

Social Media Accounts

The following is a list of favorite socials that brought me daily inspiration and hope. Safe From the Storm social accounts is one way to stay connected with me while continuing your healing journey.

1. @_safefromthestorm
2. @doyoumined (App available – access to therapists & coaches)
3. @createthelove
4. @gabormatemd
5. @brenebrown
6. @dr.alexandra.soloman
7. @corymuscara
8. @terricole
9. @najwazebian
10. @drjoedispenza
11. @davidjimeditation

Acknowledgments

This book would not be possible without the incredible ongoing support of my parents, family, friends, and loved ones. I have learned faith, perserverance, strength, and unconditional love from their example, and I couldn't be prouder of the people who surround me. Their guidance has kept me sane on days where I didn't think it was possible. They also cleaned me up, fed me, healed me, and showed me there is no such thing as failure, only a string of experiences to learn from.

There were also untold counselors, therapists, and medical professionals who were part of our healing journey. I don't have words to express my gratitude to them— not just for their services but because they gave a healing space to myself and my loved ones in the most dire and traumatic circumstances. The field of addiction isn't glamorous, but you are indeed heroes for stepping into the fray. You are so desperately needed.

Printed in Great Britain
by Amazon

73049390R00112